THE NONSTOP LOVE-IN

THE NONSTOP LOVE-IN

poems, stories, essays & other writings

David!.

peace, love & happiness

JOHNNY STALLINGS

Johnny

THE NONSTOP LOVE-IN

Open Road Press
4110 SE Hawthorne Blvd, PMB 268
Portland, OR 97214
openroadpdx.org/open-road-press/

A portion of the profits from sales of this book will be donated to Open Road Press to seed future publications.

Book design by Vinnie Kinsella, Indigo: Editing, Design, and More. www.indigoediting.com.

Cover photo by Corky Miller.

ISBN (paperback): 979-8-9898011-0-7
ISBN (ebook): 979-8-9898011-1-4

Library of Congress Control Number: 2024901652

for Nancy

Love to faults is always blind,
Always is to joy inclin'd,
Lawless, wing'd & unconfin'd,
And breaks all chains from every mind.

—William Blake

And this our life, exempt from public haunt,
Finds tongues in trees, books in the running
  brooks,
Sermons in stones, and good in every thing.

—William Shakespeare, "As You Like It"

All truths wait in all things.

—Walt Whitman, "Song of Myself"

In this world, hate never yet dispelled hate.
Only love dispels hate.
This is the law—ancient and inexhaustible.

—Buddha, *Dhammapada*

Art Degraded, Imagination Denied, War Governed the Nations.

—William Blake

To create around ourselves the kind of world that we wish to live in—isn't that the most important project of our lives?

—Slava Polunin, *Alchemy of Snowness*

None does offend. None, I say. None.

—William Shakespeare, *King Lear*

Contents

Foreword(s)

One wintery day in the 1980's, the buzzer in my New York City tenement apartment rang. The ancient intercom system never functioned, so I walked down the stairs to see who was calling. There on the stoop was Johnny Stallings. It was about 30 degrees out and snow was lightly falling, but Johnny was dressed for an Indian summer afternoon: sandals, jeans, a paisley kurta, a fringed cloth bag on his head as a hat. He had arrived at JFK Airport with twenty dollars in his pocket, and somehow he had convinced a cab driver to bring him to my address. Whenever I think of Johnny, the first image that comes to mind is this apparition: a glowing, inappropriately dressed young man with laughing eyes and a goofy grin, standing at my doorway in the snow.

The following morning I went to my office job, and Johnny headed for the public library. Johnny doesn't belong to an established religion, but the public library fills that desideratum for him. While Johnny was reading, a beautiful young woman appeared. She said, "I can see by the books you have that we are friends." She offered him her nearby apartment for a couple of weeks while she would be away. By the time I returned from work, Johnny had also acquired two jobs in the neighborhood: one in a once-famous but fading esoteric book shop, and the other in a nearby health food store.

The first time I met Johnny, I was working in a school for teenage dropouts who had exhausted all the possibilities the Portland, Oregon school system could offer. It was 1970, I was a conscientious objector, and this was my alternative service. Johnny was working for some agency that was touring social assistance programs. I remember that he asked me if I had read *Autobiography of a Yogi*, and when I said I had, he replied something like, "*That* is what I am interested in: the approach to life as joy." Johnny said that reading Paramahansa Yogananda's *Autobiography* had been like finding a door in your house that you had never noticed and that no-one had ever spoken about. Behind that door was an entirely new dimension—a possibility of imagination, magic, art, creativity, wisdom, depth and love. Johnny and I were children of the 60's. In our houses there was a door that led to Vietnam and inconceivable horror; there was a door that led to a conventional life of conformity and making money. In our different ways, Johnny and I went through the Yogananda door and we didn't look back. How could we?

Life in the 70's, 80's and beyond was theater; it was yoga and meditation; it was avant-garde films; it was be-ins and outdoor concerts, tortured romances, pancake breakfasts, and political protests. For Johnny, life involved travel to India and involvement in the world of intellectual yogis. Life was art and dance, but it was also assassinations, the endless war, Black Power, Women's Liberation, Gay Pride, and all-night philosophical discussions in coffee shops. Underlying this richness, instigating and supporting, inspiring and critiquing, illuminating and fulfilling—there were the books!

In the age of the computer, e-reader and cellphone, it is almost impossible to conjure up the prominence of "the book" as a cultural icon. There were the classics, of course, but there were also less exalted volumes that "everybody" read. The pre-boomer generation had grown up without television; they had read Shakespeare and Tennyson, and memorized poetry in high school. They passed on to the boomers the importance of reading. "Everyone" seemed to have read best selling novels, political biographies, cultural analyses, prophecies of ecological and nuclear doom, even some poetry and mysticism. This heritage was not lost on Johnny Stallings.

Johnny delights in books, he adores books, he carries their tonnage on his back with astounding ease, he swims in books which surround him as a paper sea. There is never a topic of discussion with Johnny that doesn't involve his noting at least once, "There is a book about this," or "the best book about that is…" or "you *have* to read…" If Johnny has visited me for a day or two he is able to find any book in my substantial collection, often reaching for the desired tome and page number without even looking. He calls it his "siddli"—a play on the words for an Indian rice cake, "idli," and "siddhis," the magical powers yogis are said to attain through meditation and asceticism. He has memorized and performed great swaths of Shakespeare and Whitman. He has surrounded himself with writers and readers. His friends and his partner are all readers, and he hosts a regular "Bibliophiles Unanimous!" meeting.

And so, inevitably, we come to the book you are holding in your hand.

I say inevitably because, in addition to being a voracious reader, Johnny has also been a writer all his life. Since the early days of pancake breakfasts in Portland, Johnny has written stories, plays, and poems: a celebration of the glory of the coffee bean, a play about William Blake, notes for a screenplay about some old actors robbing a bank so they could be sent to prison and act in a prison production of Hamlet (based on a conversation at a party), a play that invites the audience to join him in silent meditation—to name a few. Johnny has filled stacks of notebooks with sketches, observations and reviews; he has written countless letters, from the days when there was no alternative, up until today—when he corresponds with many prisoners and ex-prisoners that he met through his work directing plays and doing dialogue groups in Oregon prisons.

Some of this writing is here.

This is not a book to be traversed cover to cover. Lucky readers can find in it "a visit with Johnny" by leafing through its pages or scanning the table of contents and seizing on anything that looks curious, puzzling or amusing. The young man who told me he was interested in an approach to life as joy has not betrayed that interest in the 53 years that I have known him. There is fun as well as some profundity here. Just glance at a few of the titles: "Therapy" and "The Mystery of Love" are followed by "The Ambitious Peanut" and "Miracle Pancake." Some pieces were conceived decades ago, and others appeared recently in *Peace, Love, Happiness & Understanding,* or the *Open Road Meditation & Mindfulness Dialogue*—journals published by his nonprofit organization, The Open Road.

Anyone who knows Johnny has heard endless paeans to the centrality of love in sentient life. In fact, Johnny's *definition* of life has long been "The Nonstop Love-In"—echoing his hippie days and honoring the Beatles' resolution that this quality is in fact *all we need.* You will find many examples of Johnny's dedication to love in the pages that follow. Johnny is a lover and a devoted friend who has engaged in the hard work and genuine pleasure of sustaining many friendships over many decades. But I believe most "friends of Johnny" would agree with me that the shock of love that truly breaks and transforms the human heart only really came into his life through his connection with his partner, Nancy Scharbach, and his work with the men in the Two Rivers Correctional Institution in Umatilla, Oregon. There is too much to say about this, and about other influences in this direction, but for the moment I'll simply give these sentences of homage.

So: the author has asked me to write a Foreword to his book and I have done the best I can in the time available. As someone who has sometimes criticized Johnny for being didactic, I can hardly believe the tone I have fallen into writing this piece. Personally, I tend to skip Forewords and Introductions, and that is what I hope you will do. You will find so much to enjoy, so many laughs, so many ideas to consider, and so much love, it will give you a reminder or an inkling of what it is like to pass an afternoon with Johnny Stallings.

—Howard Thoresen

Here is a book I would like to read. It is funny and un-predictable. It is written by my friend Johnny Stallings. Amazing, I am reading it now. It makes me feel possible. It is warm. Something fresh happens. I am reminded of long ago when we first saw Johnny act his one man King Lear. He illuminated the words and the love in all the people of the play. Like these writings—like his life—taking joyous risks and liberating as he goes.

"Everything I touch touches me." This is the first line in Johnny's book.

He walked away from compulsory schooling and began his life of free reading, free meditation and acting. He has read immensely and has come to us distilling and offering experiments in freedom.

Rick Bartow, the painter, made beautiful portraits of Johnny acting. Once he gave Johnny a crow mask. Johnny was working as an artist's model at the time. He put on the bird mask and danced around the studio. And as he modeled it came to him to make Crow writings. In one piece that especially touches me "Crow" is miserable. "Bartow" urges him to get out of town. In the desert "Crow" trains himself to see.

In 2006 he found Nancy and she found him. He performed his one man Hamlet for men in an Oregon prison. The discussion after the play was exciting. The men wanted more. Johnny began his prison dialogues. To speak and be heard and in turn listen. This is the wonderful dignity. They asked him to direct them in

Shakespeare. Many plays followed. Much dialogue. These are his experiments. Liberation from the inside. Nancy made beautiful costumes and beautiful painted scenes. She loved the men and they her. All collaborating.

In this book there are sad mishaps among donuts, moldy cheeses that don't listen to their mothers, ants telling gruesome stories to their children and then dying, nosepickers being robbed and cuckolded. There are two poems that contain mattresses. Leaky pens imitating the sound of the rain. There are stories of failure followed by the snow falling. A fabulous quote from Emerson about the world being anything you name it. A purple crayon as great as Don Quixote. Meditation on the golden world that zig-zags among the treasures of Dostoevsky and Alice in Wonderland.

There are small poems that leave an opening for the world. I have known Johnny for 50 years and he has always urged me to open towards the world. And he continues in this book.

Thank you Johnny Stallings for all of the above and also for your love of Walt Whitman. When the earth is hurting and the people are at war Johnny is still reading Walt Whitman's poem with his heart. (Taking it in and sharing it all over the country.) The tenderness toward everyone!

—Alan Benditt

Introduction

I love books. I carry at least three books with me wherever I go. Our house is filled with books. My idea of Paradise is the Multnomah County Library. I have gotten so much pleasure from books! Books continue to change the way I see, experience and understand what's going on here.

From the time I was 17, I assumed that I would write a book. I'm 71 now. Where's the book? You're holding it in your hands.

I didn't want to write a novel of pirate adventures on the high seas—although some of the very short stories herein are just for fun. I wanted my book to share what I've learned on my life journey. I've gotten so many blessing from things that other people have written, I wanted to give a gift in return—my contribution to the Big Conversation that's been going on for a long time now.

Over the years I've had many ideas about the book I might someday write. Fairly recently, it occurred to me that I have already written My Book. All I had to do was collect some of the things I've written over the years, and publish them. Simple.

I hope that you, dear reader, are delighted from time to time, as you read these pages.

peace, love & happiness

Johnny
(written on Walt Whitman's birthday, May 31, 2023)

some small poems

A lot of these arrived while I was writing in my journal. Most of the poems in this section were written as the 20th Century was ending and the 21st Century was just beginning.

everything i touch
touches me

for crows
every day is Saturday

for Han-shan

my garret is a hut in the mountains
the stairs, an icy path which no one climbs
I sit on my futon, a white cloud
and float above this world of cares

Buildings

birds sometimes sneak into poems that aren't even
    about birds
like this one
which is about buildings

small
poem

couple of guys
unloading mattresses
from a Frito-Lay truck
what the hell is going on?

Of course Jesus is God!
How could anyone not be God?

today i'm going to hone my tea-drinking skills

all children
are our children

all these people
walking around imagining
that the ideas in their heads
make them different from each other

when you see how simple it is to be happy
you'll kick yourself
for spending so much time being miserable

My Foreign Policy

there are no foreigners

History of the World

Somewhere, at this moment, a woman is giving birth.
Meanwhile, a soldier is loading his rifle.

2 a.m.

the sound of rain on the skylight
this pen is leaking all over my fingers

no thought
no problem

thought
no problem

the Buddha's best sermon
was when he held up a flower

do you imagine
there is some other day?

some very short stories

One morning I woke up and started writing very short stories. I wrote several dozen in a few days, then stopped. This happened sometime between 2003 and 2006. Most of these are from that brief episode.

Therapy

A woman went to see her therapist, who was also a woman. "I have a problem," she began. "Yes?" the therapist said, in that way that therapists do. "It's my husband," the woman said. "I don't see your husband here," said the therapist. "He's not here," said the woman. "Where is your problem?" asked the therapist. "In my mind," the woman said, and suddenly realized highest perfect enlightenment.

The Mystery of Love

Once there was a young man who fell in love with a young woman. "Do you love me?" he asked. "If you are patient," she said, "I will answer your question." Some days went by. Some weeks. Years! One day, when they were both old and gray, the woman said, "Yes! Yes, I do love you!" "I wish you would have told me sooner," said the man.

The Ambitious Peanut

Once there was a peanut who wanted to be a writer. Her friends pooh-poohed her ambition. She wrote a story about a peanut whose aspirations to be a writer were scoffed at by her friends. When she won the Cathcart Prize for Short Fiction her friends were chagrined. Their only claim to fame was providing the inspiration for the despicable characters in this award-winning story.

Miracle Pancake

Once there was a woman who had been in an accident, lost the use of her legs, and was confined to a wheelchair. One day, as she was making a pancake, she saw the image of the Virgin Mary in the pancake. In amazement and joy, she leapt to her feet. She was healed! Word soon spread of this event, and everyone in the town, except one, came to see. A few said they could see the Virgin Mary's image quite clearly. Others said they could just barely make it out. Most said that it just looked like a pancake to them. They could all see that the woman could now walk. But there was nothing very remarkable about that. After all, they had all walked to her house to see the miracle. Most went home disappointed that they had not seen a miracle. As for the one who stayed home—she saw nonstop miracles all day long.

Non Sequitur Story

A man disembarked from a train and surveyed the platform. Which was unremarkable, since he was a surveyor. Nevertheless, someone remarked on it. In front of the train station, a mangy dog was rolling around in something unsavory. A flock of pigeons took flight. Down the street a poltroon was beating his young son with a razor strop for some nominal offense. An otiose gentleman went for his morning constitutional. It was a day that lacked promise—burdened, as it was, by all the failures, cruelties and prevarications that preceded it. I woke at last from a seemingly endless dream, in which I was being chased by knife-wielding thugs. I made myself a cup of coffee and wondered how I was going to summon the courage to face another day at the vitamin factory.

Of Jack, Who Seldom Laughed

He poured himself another drink and stared uncomprehendingly at the hand which Fate had dealt him. He knew the time had come to move forward and yet he stood frozen to the spot. He couldn't understand why water seemed to slip through his fingers, leaving him with the taste of ashes in his mouth. He was like a ship that had run aground on the shoals of undreamt possibilities. A keen sense of the futility of all his efforts ripped through his guts like a knife. He rubbed the sleep from his eyes and took a penny from a blind man's cup. Since childhood he had always longed to prove something to his father, who abandoned his mother before he could get her pregnant. For her part, she swore an oath never to swear oaths, and raised Jack—for that was his name—on a strict diet of cold oatmeal and luscious fruits, fed to him by Tahitian maidens, who were renting the spare bedroom. And so his life would have continued in a more-or-less normal way had Chance not intervened in the guise of a mysterious and unexpected event. No sooner had doubt sealed his lips, than he began to yearn for something he could never quite possess. This made his yearning all the more poignant. The tempest which raged within the teacup of his cranium would not abate until he found someone who could share his bewilderment at life's inexplicable vagaries. Little did he know that his dream of finding a soulmate would be interrupted by a loud knocking at the door. He turned over and tried to go back to sleep, but it was no use! A painful memory surged up from the depths of his very being. It was the memory of a humiliating night spent in a phone booth at a busy intersection, wearing only a pair of mismatched socks. Needless to say, he reproached himself for all the big and little ways he had betrayed the trust of those who needed him most. He felt that if only he could put the shoe on the other foot he would better understand the steps that had led him into a slough of despond. But his slim hopes for a brighter tomorrow were dashed when an industrial accident robbed him of his eyesight and left him stone deaf into the bargain. He tried to console himself with thoughts of frolicking kittens, but soon tired of this diversion. He spent his remaining years trying to convince passersby that charitable acts never go unrewarded, but in this, too, he enjoyed little success.

Snow

One night, when everyone was sleeping, it snowed!
The falling snow didn't make a sound.

Playing

Once there was a woman who played hard to get. Another played the accordion.

The Ocean

Once there was a little fish who asked her mother: "Where's the ocean?"

some attempts (essays)

From time to time I like to share my thoughts with an imaginary reader.

Battle or Picnic?

"The world is a Dancer; it is a Rosary; it is a Torrent; it is a Boat; a Mist; a Spider's Snare: it is what you will; and the metaphor will hold, and it will give the imagination keen pleasure. Swifter than light the world converts itself into the thing you name, and all things find their right place under this new and capricious classification. Must I call the heaven and the earth a maypole and country fair with booths, or an anthill, or an old coat, in order to give you the shock of pleasure which the imagination loves and the sense of spiritual greatness? Call it a blossom, a rod, a wreath of parsley, a tamarisk-crown, a cock, a sparrow, the ear instantly hears and the spirit leaps to the trope."

—from *The Journals of Ralph Waldo Emerson*,
edited by Linscott, pp. 197-198, (1841)

Life has often been described as a battle. Perhaps the most famous example is the Bhagavad Gita. Just as a great battle is about to begin, the warrior-prince Arjuna asks his charioteer and guru, the god Krishna, to drive their chariot between the two armies. Time stops. Filled with pity, and unwilling to kill his kinsmen who are on the opposing side, Arjuna refuses to fight. Krishna urges Arjuna to do his duty, to stand up and fight like a man. He teaches Arjuna that the highest liberation comes from the realization that one's self is the unborn and undying Self of all—not other than God. Arjuna decides to join the fight, the battle begins, and everyone on both sides is slaughtered.

The Bhagavad Gita is a complex wisdom text which is located in the middle of a story about war. It is essentially about yoga and how to live a life of inner peace and freedom, but the plot of the epic in which it is set requires Arjuna to fight in the war. So, a central metaphor suggests that life is a battle, and the honorable thing is to boldly do what is required of you.

We are often reminded that life is a struggle or a battle. Darwin's idea of the survival of the fittest is used to support this idea. Our economic system is predicated on the idea of a fierce competition which many people will inevitably lose. Too bad for them.

I like the Buddhist teacher Thich Nhat Hanh. In one of his talks at a meditation retreat, he began by saying: "Some people think that a meditation retreat is a kind of picnic…" When someone is an expert in a field, he usually warns newcomers that such expertise requires years of discipline and hard work. So, I was expecting Thich Nhat Hanh to continue by saying, "…but it's not." He surprised me by next saying: "I love picnics!"

And I thought to myself: "I love picnics, too! Everyone loves picnics! Picnics are lovely!"

It occurred to me that rather than thinking of life as a struggle, as some kind of ordeal, as a battle to be fought, I would think of my life as a picnic. Why not? As we learn from Ralph Waldo Emerson's entertaining epigram that I am using as the epigraph for this essay, we can say anything we want. I have the feeling that life is everything-at-once. But I can't imagine everything-at-once. So, for now, I'm going with "picnic."

It's a picnic to which everyone is invited. A gathering. A feast. Little kids are running around. Maybe there's a softball game. There's potato salad. Sandwiches. Lemonade. There might be pie. Ants. At a picnic, everyone has the feeling that life is good.

Since we're here just a little while, doesn't that sound good? As a metaphor, isn't it preferable to a scene of chaos, confusion and carnage?

In the UNESCO Constitution, signed in November of 1945, it says: "…wars begin in the minds of men…" We should choose our metaphors wisely.

Walt & Me

I'm not a scholar. I dropped out of college after half a year, way back in 1969. I wasn't introduced to Walt Whitman by an English Professor, but by Walt himself, when I was seventeen or eighteen years old. And that has made all the difference.

Walt Whitman is my friend. He is a companion on my life's journey on the open road. I love him. And I know that he loves me. I can prove it with a simple syllogism. Walt Whitman loves everyone. I am someone. Therefore, Walt Whitman loves me.

No doubt the critical writings about Walt Whitman and his poetry and prose are vast. I haven't read them. Well, maybe a few things here and there. I *have* read "Song of Myself" over and over and over again for fifty years.

I memorized most of the poem—a version I edited down to an hour in length—and have performed it publicly many times, from Portland to Bainbridge Island to New York City to Marfa, Texas to Guanajuato, Mexico to Two Rivers prison in Umatilla, Oregon. The Grand Tour!

When you perform a play or a long poem—sometimes, as in the case of King Lear, it's the same thing—you have to "run your lines" a lot in preparation for the performance, so that you don't screw it up. You say the words aloud. You must mean what you say. You must feel the feelings. You must believe that what you say is true.

One of the striking things about "Song of Myself" is that it is written in the first person. When Walt says "I believe a leaf of grass is no less than the journey-work of the stars...And a mouse is miracle enough to stagger sextillions of infidels," if you were analyzing the poem in a classroom, you might say, "Whitman believed that a blade of grass was somehow equivalent to the movement of the stars. He thought mice were amazing." But if you say the words aloud to someone who is listening to you, or stand on a hilltop and say them to the four directions—if you mean what you say, and feel the feelings, and believe what you are saying is true, then something will happen to you.

Walt knew this. In the Introduction to the first edition, in 1855, of his self-published book of twelve poems titled *Leaves of Grass*, which included the (then untitled) poem "Song of Myself," he said this:

> ...read these leaves in the open air every season of every year of your life,...and your very flesh shall be a great poem and have the richest fluency not only in its words but in the silent lines of its lips and face and between the lashes of your eyes and in every motion and joint of your body.

I have performed the experiment, and I know that what he says is true.

—written on Walt Whitman's 201st birthday,
May 31st, 2020

Harold and the Purple Crayon

The world is so full of a number of things.
I'm sure we should all be as happy as kings.

—"Happy Thought," by Robert Louis
Stevenson, from *A Child's Garden of Verses*

Among the great works of imaginative literature,
along with *The Odyssey* of Homer, Dante's *Divina
Commedia*, Cervantes' *Don Quixote*, Shakespeare's *A
Midsummer Night's Dream* and Dostoevsky's *Brothers
Karamazov*, we must place Crockett Johnson's *Harold
and the Purple Crayon*. As a philosophical vision, it
stands beside the *Bhagavad Gita*, Plato's "Allegory of
the Cave," and Wittgenstein's *Logisch-philosophische
Abhandlung*. When we think of works of visual art
to which we might compare it, several come to mind:
"The Adoration of of the Mystic Lamb" by Hubert and
Jan van Eyck (1432), "The Garden of Earthly Delights"
by Hieronymus Bosch (1510), Michelangelo's fresco on
the ceiling of the Sistine Chapel (1512), "The Isenheim
Altarpiece" by Nikolaus of Haguenau and Matthias
Grünewald (1516), and perhaps Pablo Picasso's
"Guernica" (1937).

In Crockett Johnson's masterpiece, young Harold, dressed in those kind of flannel pajamas into which you put your feet ("onesies"), sets out like Parsifal on an epic journey, armed only with a purple crayon. As he goes, he creates the world in which he lives. He makes a moon, so he will have moonlight to light his way. He terrifies himself with a monster from his own id. He falls into a sea of his own making, but saves himself from drowning by drawing a boat with his purple crayon and climbing into it. I'll say no more of what befalls our youthful protagonist on his quest. Suffice it to say that, as in the archetypal Hero's Journey, he returns home with a Treasure, and bestows it upon Humanity. The Treasure is of course the slender tome: *Harold and the Purple Crayon*.

My Imaginary TED Talk

Be kind whenever possible. It is always possible.

—Dalai Lama

I haven't been asked to give a TED talk, but the other day I was thinking about what I would say if I *was* asked. Here's what I wrote:

> Love to faults is always blind,
> Always is to joy inclin'd,
> Lawless, wing'd & unconfin'd,
> And breaks all chains from every mind.

that's William Blake

I'd like to talk about love

and so I shall

not the fascinating question of the relation between love and sex

but another kind of love:

unconditional love for everyone and every thing

is such a love possible?

that's an open question

but surely it is possible to have this as an aspiration

for our love to grow and grow as we go along on our
life journey

it is good to begin with this axiom:

we are one human family

that means:

all children are our children

all children are our children

every child, everywhere in the world

if you accept this as true, then war becomes impossible

unthinkable

for whenever we drop a bomb on our so-called "enemies" we would at the same time murder some of our own children

surely we don't want to do that

it's much more pleasant to have no enemies

there's no one to fear

we can live in love

the preamble to the UNESCO constitution says:

"wars begin in the minds of men"

so, that's where they must end, too

we can end the wars within ourselves

by doing our own inner work

the other kind of war—between nations and groups of people—

ends with acts of imagination, informed by love

by the knowledge that each person's life is as limitless
and precious as our own

if we don't imagine that we have enemies, we don't
have enemies

this is true, because we are one human family

and all children are our children

we have no enemies

there is no "other"

there is no scapegoat upon whom to project all our sins

we are not born in sin

(every newborn baby proves Saint Augustine was
wrong about that)

we are born in love

we grow in love

that's why we came here

to love and be loved

that's why we came to this earth

that's why we came to this room

love has no limit

it has no beginning or end

to quote the Bible:

who loves not, knows not God

for God is love

Jesus enjoined us to love our neighbors as ourselves

and to love our enemies

if you love your enemies, they are no longer enemies

they are friends

brothers and sisters

* * *

our family is larger than the human family

it includes every living being

and rocks and rivers and clouds

Thich Nhat Hanh speaks of interbeing

we all inter-are

the trees provide oxygen for us to breathe

each of our bodies is a host for millions of micro-organisms, without which we couldn't digest our food

it's wonderful!

whether or not you postulate a creator, this world is amazing!

every particle of creation is miraculous

everywhere you look is another miracle

our breath, the circulation of our blood, our brain, the bees pollinating the fruit trees—

the Web of Life!

the odds against any one of us being born are impos-
sibly large—

the chance meeting of our parents, the moment of
conception, the zillions of little swimmers—

and yet here we are

it is great good fortune

here we are with our precious human bodies and brains

our thoughts, our emotions, our imaginings

we are in this well-lit room, where the temperature is
regulated for our comfort

we are all suitably clothed

well-fed

we are very fortunate

many people, as we know, are not so fortunate

everyone should have access to clean and abundant

drinking water

no one should go to bed hungry

no one should live in fear

we have a lot of work to do

compassion is the essential prerequisite

* * *

the earth is hurting, too

we have been relentlessly destroying the ecological health of our planet—especially since the advent of the Industrial Revolution

we have to learn, or re-learn, how to live on this earth in ways that are not so destructive

this, too, begins with love

we must love our Mother Earth

* * *

the Beatles said:

"all you need is love"

the poet Auden said:

"we must love one another or die"

of course you probably got the memo that we're all going to die anyway

we are mortal beings

the question is:

how shall we live?

may I have the envelope please?

and the answer to the question "How shall we live?" is…

in Love

thank you

Why I Dropped Out of College

I never liked school. From Second Grade onward, I hated it. To this day, I don't know what my crime was, why I was sentenced to that confinement for years on end.

Both of my parents were college graduates with advanced degrees. My dad was a high school teacher. They always assumed that my sister and I would go to college, and told us that they would pay our tuition. In my family, education—and report cards!—were a big deal. Not much effort was required to maintain good grades, and I entered Portland State University in the Fall of 1969 in the Honors Program.

The Woodstock Festival had just happened in mid-August. There was a lot of ferment against the Vietnam War on the PSU campus. College girls were "on the pill"—the birth control pill. I was a bona fide pacifist and hippie. I only signed up for classes that sounded interesting to me. I took a course in "Deviant Personalities in Literature" from the notorious Joe Uris. The most popular course on campus that Fall was taught by a student, Dan Wolfe. Its title was: "Is Man Dead?"

As interesting as this might have been, for me all the excitement was happening outside the classroom. I had been sitting in classrooms since the age of six. The windowless hallways of the school had the cheerless aspect of a mental hospital. I went to meetings of the Students for a Democratic Society. I helped organize demonstrations to get military recruiters off the campus. In October and November of 1969, in Portland and cities across the country there were Moratoriums to End the War in Vietnam—the largest anti-war demonstrations in history. Along with four other PSU students, I was put on "disciplinary probation" for my anti-war activities. I was one of the notorious Portland State Five!

The Summer after I graduated from high school, I read *On the Road* and *The Dharma Bums* by Jack Kerouac. A call to adventure was beckoning me. I had the epiphany that going to school was no longer mandatory, and I heeded the call.

As I walked away from school, I felt free. I felt a great surge of joy! I still have a recurring dream of walking out of a school building and feeling glorious, although in my dreams I am walking out of Maplewood Elementary School or Wilson High School—something that seemed impossible to me at the time.

As the poet said, if you take the road less travelled it makes all the difference. Joseph Campbell recommends entering the forest where there is no path or way, like the knights of the Round Table, if you want to have the authentic adventures that only you can have. The Unplanned Life has a richness and variety that I cherish. If peace, love and happiness count for anything, I am as fortunate as anyone on earth.

On Not Living in Trumplandia

Trumplandia is an imaginary kingdom by the sea. The god and emperor of Trumplandia is a wealthy aging celebrity, a television personality, whose strange misfortune it was to get elected President of the United States of America. He did this by telling everyone that he would make America great again, but the odd thing about it is that he didn't even live in America. He lived in a fantastical world of his own imagining. He was the kind of mythical creature who gets bigger and bigger every time someone says his name. And since every day people everywhere repeated his name again and again, he got bigger and bigger and bigger. Some thought he would devour the world. But a more likely fate for him would be that of the unfortunate gentleman in the Monty Python film "The Meaning of Life," who ate and ate and ate and got bigger and bigger and bigger until he exploded.

Members of the media are forced to wander the labyrinth of Trumplandia every day and report back to the rest of us what is going on there. It is not a happy place. And yet people could not help tuning in for the latest dispatches from Trumplandia until everyone was magically transported to the kingdom, whether they liked it or not, and were unable to escape. In Trumplandia everything is always about the latest thing that the god-emperor has said. He tweets decrees in the middle of the night, nonsensical ravings, and yet everyone in Trumplandia can talk of nothing else.

I know this to be true, because I was once a prisoner in Trumplandia. This is a call to the people who are enslaved in Trumplandia: Escape! Escape! There are other worlds, beautiful worlds waiting for you. You are trapped in someone else's nightmare. Wake up! There is beauty, truth and goodness outside those prison walls. Children play. There is love and laughter. Miracles abound!

In the kingdom of hatred and anger and fear a dark cloud hides the sun. People wander in hopelessness and despair. But the spell can be broken. Just as the angry man lives in a world of assholes, so the happy woman lives in a world of friendly people. You only have to imagine yourself somewhere else and you are no longer in Trumplandia. Imagine kindness, compassion, generosity, freedom.

Again and again the media wizards and even your friends will capture you and drag you back to Trumplandia. But in each moment there is the possibility of escape, the possibility of freedom. In the Real World, the Golden World, the god-emperor of Trumplandia has no power. In the Golden World, Love is the law, and that which does not obey the eternal law of Love perishes.

The dark fantasies of violence and greed are smoke. Life abides from everlasting to everlasting.

Slowness

Eighteen years ago I was living in a small homesteader's cabin in Central Oregon. One day I was chopping vegetables, preparing a meal with great efficiency, when for some reason, or no reason, I suddenly slowed down. Instead of moving rapidly from cutting board to stove, I walked s-l-o-w-l-y. And something happened. It was quiet. I hadn't noticed it, but my mind had been busy with something or other, while I was busy preparing dinner. Now I wasn't "preparing dinner." As I took each step, my bare feet felt the floor. It felt like a blessing to be walking, to be alive. The broccoli was beautiful. Everything was perfect.

I have performed this experiment thousands of times since then. I know that if I slow down I see what I'm looking at. I taste what I'm eating. Every thing is beautiful. Perfect.

Reading Less and Less
While Collecting More and More Books

I don't know why this is happening. As I get older, I read less and less. Nevertheless, I continue to collect books at an alarming rate. I'm never going to read them all! For every hundred books I check out from the library, I might read one. Something like that. What's going on here? What does this mean?

I don't know. Speaking of not knowing, I seem to know less and less, rather than more and more. I don't have much faith in what I do pretend to know. This may sound like an unpleasant experience. But the truth of the matter is that I enjoy not knowing. I take pleasure in the vastness of my ever-expanding ignorance.

I have suffered my whole life—and, more poignantly, made other people suffer—by pretending to be Mr. Know-It-All. As I shed the responsibilities that go with that noxious role, I feel a great sense of relief. When people ask me a question, I say: "Ask Mr. Google. He knows everything."

I read a little bit and I'm sated. I'm like someone who used to pile his plate high at one of those all-you-can-eat buffets who now just orders a small salad. A few bites and I'm content. A few words, and I'm good. (This is just a metaphor. At an all-you-can-eat buffet, I'm one of those people who piles his plate high.) I often find myself surrounded by books with no desire to open any of them.

At other times I find myself intrigued by all those unread books. Someone will casually mention the name of an author. I think to myself: "I haven't read anything by that author." Then, I log onto the Multnomah County Library website and put not one, but at least five books by that author "on hold." Over the next days and weeks the books arrive, but by that time I have once again decided to read everything I can about treehouses or Greek Mythology. My interest in Greek Mythology doesn't last long, because I decide I need to improve my Spanish. It's been a long time since I read William Blake's "The Marriage of Heaven and Hell" or Shelley's "Defense of Poetry." I haven't even read *Frankenstein* yet! Or *Sense and Sensibility*!

I try to avoid big thick books altogether, but they sneak up on me when I'm not looking. At the moment, I'm slowly making my way through *Horizon* by Barry Lopez—512 pages! Don't get me wrong. It's a great book. I read slowly, because these days I rarely read anything for long stretches at a time. There are other things to do in life besides reading books!

I have long imagined that one day I would write a great book and present it as my gift to humanity. The thing is, I want to be a famous author without all the hard work of actually writing and re-writing. Because I don't seem to have whatever it takes to stay concentrated for long periods of time—(and it's getting worse)—my best go, I think, is to write in little bursts and somehow collect the best of the bursts into some kind of book.

I can say with some confidence that it's very unlikely that I will ever write a novel that resembles *War and Peace*. (Another book I haven't read.) I frankly admit that I am no Leo Tolstoy. But that doesn't mean that I might not cobble together some words that bring delight, or even—(dream on!)—edification to my fellow mortals. I'm not dead yet!

a poem

This one is a little too long to be considered a small poem.

let's pretend

instead of pretending that we are afraid
that we must improve
that we have enemies
that the future will arrive someday

let's pretend everything is sacred
pretend this is Paradise
pretend every moment is precious
pretend we love everyone

pretend our joy knows no bounds
pretend we are the whole wide world

a theater piece

I've performed a number of short (and long) works by writers like William Shakespeare, Fyodor Dostoevsky & Johnny Stallings. This is one of mine. It's not as dramatic as King Lear, but I performed it in front of people, so I call it a theater piece.

Goldfinches!

a theatrical monologue

this is a story about stories

and about something that we might call "the storyless state"

joseph campbell wrote a book called *the hero with a thousand faces* about a kind of story that is found throughout history and all over the world that he called "the hero's journey"

we can use the hero's journey as a metaphor for our life

and i would like to use it as the structure for this evening's entertainment

the hero's journey begins with the call to adventure

we have all already answered the call to adventure by coming here tonight

we could have stayed home and watched tv

but instead we left the comfort and safety and security of our homes—for what?

we don't know

and that is where the hero journeys: into the unknown

into a dark wood, or a cave, or to the bottom of the sea

one of the main things about the unknown is that you don't know what you will find

i answered the call to adventure by deciding to write and perform a theatrical monologue

why would i want to undertake such a thing?

that brings me to a little story about my life...

when i graduated from high school, i went to college just like i was supposed to

but i had never liked school

it always felt like a prison to me

and one day i realized that going to school was optional

and i could opt not to go

which i did

now that is the age when you are supposed to choose a career and get with the program

but i graduated from high school in 1969, during the hippie era

we are very prone to conformity at that age—maybe throughout life—and somehow i found myself conforming to the hippie form of "non-conformity"

with long hair and oddball clothing and bare feet and all that

that was how i wanted to present myself to the world

i felt more at home in this costume than in a white shirt, suit and tie

now, "hippie" is not really a career choice and in fact, i neglected to choose an occupation

i've held a variety of odd jobs—i once spent 18 months testing beet pulp pellets for hardness, durability and fine particle content

for many years i found the familiar question "what do you do?" to be difficult to answer now that i'm old, i can look back on my life and ask: "what is my job?"

or, better yet, "what did i come here to do?"

and the answer, i think—or at least one answer is: to gather people together

and so that is why i had the hare-brained idea of writing and performing a theatrical monologue

it's a trick to get people to gather together

and here we are

so, what happens after the hero answers the call to adventure?

he or she goes into the wilderness—the unknown—on a quest for something

and sometimes you know what you are seeking and sometimes you don't

but in the unknown you always find *something*

and typically, the hero encounters obstacles or difficulties and meets magic helpers

and finds a treasure—which is probably guarded by a dragon or something

and the hero kills the dragon or at least tricks it

and steals the treasure

and returns home with something of value—not just for himself or herself—but for everyone

now here's an interesting thing: each one of us has treasure within

each one of us *is* the treasure

so, why do we have to go down into a cave or to the bottom of the sea to find it?

well, that's a good question

here's a story that is found in many cultures:

before we are born, we have a special gift

and in the process of being born, we lose the gift

and it is our task to find out what our gift is and then give it to everyone

for example, you might have a gift of music

and not know it

and you need to discover that you have it before you can share it with others

but if you do, your gift blesses everyone

another version of this story is:

when we are born, we forget who we are

and who we are is god

and we have to re-discover this

we have to remember what has been forgotten

the greek word for this is "anamnesis"—remembering what has been forgotten

so that is one version of our hero's journey—we have to go to the bottom of the sea, or to the first unitarian church, or wherever, to remember who we are and we have to do this every day

going to sleep every night is like dying

and every morning we wake up and it's a new day

we have been reborn

and it's great if we were happy yesterday, but it doesn't
really help us to be happy today

and we need to find happiness today

and what worked yesterday will not work today

we have to try something new

and where is the new found?

in the unknown

and so, in a way, we all may have thought we were
coming here just to entertain or be entertained, but
actually we came here because we have to save our
own life

we have to be reborn

now, as the storyteller, or entertainer, it's supposed to be my job to come up with something really fantastic

you know, the greatest theatrical monologue you've ever heard, or whatever

but i'm not too worried about that, because, as far as i'm concerned, i've already done my job, which is to gather us together

and i don't have to bring a great treasure, because you are, we are, the treasure

and i have a kind of foolproof method of creating a magical, fantastic, wonderful experience, which is: at the end of my monologue, we will have a dialogue

and a dialogue circle cannot fail to be a perfect thing

and so i'd like to reassure anyone who is worried that this evening will be something less than perfect—that is not gonna happen!

it's gonna be perfect

because however lame or inadequate my "entertaining" monologue is, we will all have an opportunity to remedy that together in the dialogue circle okay, back to our hero's journey, which is our journey into story and storylessness

william butler yeats said that each person has their own myth and that one of your jobs as a poet, or just as a human being, is to find out what your myth is

that goes back to the idea of remembering what has been forgotten

i'd like to talk about a couple kinds of stories, which i call:

identity and mythos

identity refers to the stories we tell ourselves about who we are

and mythos refers to our stories about the world

now i am going to tell you a little story about my mythos

many years ago, when i was young, i read a story by fyodor dostoevsky called "the dream of a ridiculous man"

i loved the story

it resonated with me, as they say

here's the story:

there's a guy who is depressed

life has no meaning for him

he feels that nothing makes any difference

he decides to kill himself

he buys a gun

he's just waiting for the right moment to do the deed

one night he's walking home and he sees a star in the sky and decides: "tonight is the night"

but then a little girl comes up to him and wants his help

her mother is dying or is in some very bad situation and the little girl is crying and trying to get this guy to come with her

but he doesn't help the little girl

he goes home so that he can commit suicide

but he can't get the little girl out of his mind

and he feels that he has to figure something out before he dies

and while he's sitting there, trying to figure it all out he falls asleep and dreams a dream

this is his dream:

he dreams that he kills himself

and he goes to another planet, which is like earth, except that it is paradisal

there is no fear or war or hatred

it is a world where everyone lives in love

and in his dream he ruins everything in this perfect world

he brings about a fall, very much like what happens in the story of adam and eve

the love planet gets worse and worse until it resembles our own then he wakes up

and he has a very strong feeling that he has seen the truth—that our life could be completely transformed, it could be perfect, if only we would love each other

that's dostoevsky's story

i liked it so much that i decided to perform it

but it seemed too short for an evening in the theater, so i added a piece that i had written called "columbus"

i wrote columbus in 1992, for the 500th anniversary of columbus' first voyage to the western hemisphere

i grew up with the story that columbus was a great hero who had discovered america

in my version there's this guy who is drunk and he claims to be christopher columbus

it isn't explained whether this man is delusional, or if he is the spirit of christopher columbus, back from the dead, or what

anyhow, this christopher columbus is self-medicating with alcohol because he is in a lot of pain

in his version, he didn't discover anything—people already lived here

they were a beautiful people—the taino—and they lived without war, in a kind of paradise

and he brought about a fall

the taino are no more

and my blubbering drunken christopher columbus wanted everyone to know that he had seen and understood something—that people can be beautiful and innocent and loving

he had seen it with his own eyes

and it was only after i had put these two pieces together that i realized that they had the same theme:

paradise, fall, and a vision of a possible return to paradise

and i thought: "maybe this is my myth"

people tend to think of paradise as something that may have existed in the past, or which might exist in the future—maybe even after we die but paradise, it seems to me, is this world in which we live—just as it is

this gathering is paradise

and everyone sitting here is perfect

is paradise

so it seems to me

this is my mythos—the story i tell myself about the world

now it may be objected: "how can this world be paradise when it is so full of suffering and pain?"

good question

instead of arguing whether the world is perfect or terribly flawed, i would like to explore the sense in which the world is perfect

imagine, for a moment, a goldfinch

a goldfinch is perfect

a goldfinch does not need to be improved

the very idea is absurd

everything is like the goldfinch

each one of us is a goldfinch

perfect

this is my thesis

my mythos

um, so where are we on our hero's journey this evening?

okay, so you answered the call to adventure by coming here

and your guide, your magic helper, on this journey through the dark wood of this evening is me

an unreliable guide!

and now we're lost!

but according to the unreliable guide, the trickster-helper, that's okay according to me, getting lost is a perfectly acceptable variant of the hero's journey

let's take an example from *alice in wonderland*

alice says that she feels like maybe she's lost and wonders which path she should take

and the cheshire cat asks her where she is going

and she replies that she doesn't know

and he says: "then it doesn't matter which path you take"

and that's kind of like us

except that we don't need to get anywhere, because we are already here

that's another common story theme

the bold adventurer travels the world and ends up returning home and finding the treasure under his or her own hearth

hearth equals heart

that's where our treasure is

not far away

and what is the point of this theatrical monologue?

it is to go forth and return home

to the silence which preceded the story

the world is always larger than our picture of the world

our descriptions and explanations are like cartoons

it's like the difference between looking at a postcard of
multnomah falls and standing in front of multnomah
falls

or as mark twain said: the difference between the light-
ning bug and the lightning

in this analogy, my "entertaining" theatrical mono-
logue is the lightning bug

and what is the lightning?

you are the lightning

i am the lightning

the lightning is us—just as we are

words are useful in reminding us of the inadequacy
of words

the gold that each of us came here to find, whether we
knew it or not, is each other

we tend to believe that the stories we tell ourselves
are true

the friendly person lives in a friendly world

the fearful person lives in a dangerous world

we imagine a world and then we live in that world

and who is the person who lives in this imagined world?

i think it works something like this:

when we are born, we cannot speak or understand
what people are saying to us

but very quickly we get the hang of it, and by the time we are four—even earlier—we are quite fluent in speaking and understanding the language that our parents speak

as we grow up we learn whether we are a boy or a girl, whether we are smart or stupid, whether we are beautiful or unattractive, whether great things are expected of us, or whether we'll never amount to much

by our early twenties we should have everything figured out:

we might be a beautiful republican woman

or an angry environmentalist

we could be a skater, a scientist, or a sinner

a buddhist, a baptist, an atheist, a plumber, a poet, or a certified public accountant

we might be fat, depressed, friendly, ambitious, lazy, sexy, shy, anxious, optimistic, pessimistic

but whatever we have become, whatever we believe, we are sort of stuck with it it's impressive and amazing that we can create an identity and a mythos

it's absolutely necessary that we do this

but it becomes a kind of prison, from which it seems there is no escape

we are fictional characters, living in fictional worlds of our own creation

end of story?

well, sort of

because this is prelude to the storyless state

in addition to our very impressive ability to think and to speak, we have the wonderful ability to be still

to be awake and alert

each one of us is nourished by a silence that has no beginning or end

not confined within our descriptions, explanations, thoughts, memories, stories and imaginings fearless, loving, carefree

not *in* the world, we *are* the world

a world beyond our ken

where everything and everyone is miraculous

perfect

like a raincloud, a stone

a goldfinch

thank you

some Crow stories

In my younger days, I used to model for artists—mostly in art schools. A photography student asked me to bring things that had special meaning for me. I brought a crow mask that my friend Rick Bartow had carved. I put on the mask and danced around for the photographer. As I was dancing, I wondered: "Who is this guy with the head of a bird and the body of a man?" And I started making up stories in my head about Birdman, or Crow.

Old Crow

No one knows the parentage of Crow.

But he must be very old.

He says that he was around before the sun and moon.

He says that he has seen many suns come and go.

That the universe has been created and destroyed many
times.

He has watched it all from the branches of a great
tree, he says.

And he says that everything is always changing.

Crow is changing, too.

At the end of every cosmic cycle he loses a feather.

Someday he'll be completely bald.

Eggs

Crow claims that he is the ancestor of birds and
humans.

It would be hard to prove one way or another, but he
does have the head of a bird and the body of a man.

Crow claims that a long time ago he lived in a great
tree and that he laid the egg from which the universe
was hatched.

If you point out that male crows can't lay eggs, he says
that they used to be able to.

If you ask him who laid the egg out of which he was
hatched, Crow changes the subject.

Fun

A long time ago everyone was morose.
One day, Crow invented fun.
Things have been a lot better ever since.

Corn and Bean People

Crow told this story:

Once there was a beautiful green valley with a river
    running through it.
The people in the valley grew corn and beans.
They worked hard at farming, and they were good at it.
Every year the harvest was abundant.

Some other people lived in the mountains, some dis-
    tance from the valley.
They spent their time forging swords.
They practiced fighting a lot.
They were proud and fierce warriors.

One day the people from the mountains put on their
    helmets, took up their swords, and went to the
    valley where the people who grew corn and beans
    lived.
They killed the men and raped the women and took
    all the corn and beans.

The people in the valley spent all their time farming
    and practicing the arts and crafts of self-sufficiency.
They didn't have swords.
They didn't know the first thing about fighting.
They were defenseless against the mountain people.

When the warriors got home they threw a wild party.
They ate roasted meat, with bean soup and corn on
  the cob.
They all got drunk and bragged about their heroic
  deeds.

The expedition had been exciting and fun and they all
  considered it a tremendous success.

Crow was quiet for quite a while.
Then he continued:

I've always been one of the corn and bean people.
I've never been able to understand what's going on in
  the hearts and minds of those guys with the swords.

The City and the Desert

Crow was living in the city.

His life was hectic and chaotic.

He was practically out of his mind, but he didn't even
    know it.

And the people around him didn't notice either, because
    their lives were as chaotic and crazy as Crow's.

One day Crow's friend Bartow came for a visit.

Bartow lived near the ocean.

Made masks and music and other stuff.

Bartow said: "You're a wreck!

Why don't you get away from this for awhile?"

So Crow did.

He went to the desert.

He took off his clothes and sat on a big rock.

It was hot.

Crow listened.

It was still.

He looked around.

The sky was huge.

Things weren't all crowded together, like in the city.

Crow noticed each thing.

And he took the time to appreciate each thing he saw,
    or touched.

After awhile the noise inside his head quieted down
    and the world came alive.

Crow stayed there a long time.

When Crow returned to the city he tried to bring the
    silence with him.
But it wasn't long before the noise of the city swallowed
    his silence and he was crazy again.
So he went back to the desert.
This happened over and over.
Then, one day when Crow was in the city, everything
    changed.
He looked around with new eyes.
Ugly things were beautiful.
The noise had become a kind of music.
Each moment and everything that happened filled him
    with delight.

letter to Rocky

From 2006 to 2019, I directed plays and facilitated weekly three-hour-long dialogues in Oregon prisons. Many of the men and women I met in prison are out of prison now. Some are still inside. One of my pen pals is Rocky Hutchinson. We have written a lot of letters to each other. This is the first one I wrote to him.

May 22, 2015

Dear Rocky,

Nancy and I really enjoyed getting your letter. It sounds like your life is really blossoming.

I'm glad you are enjoying the Krishnamurti book and the book by Alan Watts. I love books! It's weird how much a person would miss, growing up in our culture, if they just went to school, watched TV and popular movies, and played video games. For me, people like Krishnamurti and Thich Nhat Hanh have expanded the way I see the world and other people. Krishnamurti is especially good on the subject of freedom. Thich Nhat Hanh says important things about lovingkindness, interbeing, and peace. There is nothing about these ideas in the New York Times or The Oregonian. Nothing on the evening news. Nothing in school. And yet they are so important! As it turns out, a lot of people are talking about these things, but you need to find them!

It's as if people live in different worlds. Some live in worlds of anger and sorrow and fear. Others live in love. And peace. And joy. Many people don't know that they have a choice about all this. I think you have figured it out. Congratulations!

peace, love & happiness
Johnny

some more small poems

Here are more small poems—mostly born while writing in my journal. I wrote a lot of these while living in a cabin in a very very small town in Central Oregon, from 2003 to 2006. The last few are more recent.

last night i was playing miniature golf in my dream

a guy drives by in a blue car
covered with cherry blossom petals

hey, don't quarrel!
there's plenty of birdseed for everyone

My Retirement Plan

(written on my 53rd birthday)

I'm waiting for the elves to arrive
with bags of gold

Christmas Prayer

Thank you, Jesus
for giving me this day off work.

cold night
sitting by the woodstove
the happiest man alive

a bowl of oatmeal
and a cup of coffee
did you think heaven was up in the sky somewhere?

found poem

this production contains light atmospheric mist
and includes a loud noise at the end of act one

Y'know those paperweights
with a little house
and little trees
and if you turn it upside-down
and then rightside-up again
it snows?
I'm sitting in that little house.

i live in Paradise
but am unable to enjoy the suffering of the damned

when water touches the tongue
something happens!
all the scientists in the world
will never figure out what that is

alone in his room
why is this man smiling?

living in silence
big wind

there is so much
i don't know

if you want to find happiness in this life

plant flowers that attract hummingbirds

the other shore
beneath our feet

there has never been
is not now
and will never be
anything more perfect
than this glass of water

i am thankful
that i got to come to this planet
and eat a mango

pandemic poem

someone forgot to tell Spring
to stay home

peace, love & happiness in the anthropocene

just because the world as we knew it
is coming to an end
it's no reason not to enjoy
this beautiful day

My Foolproof Plan for World Peace

I hereby declare today to be International Love Day.
And a General Armistice.
All hostilities must cease on International Love Day.
Henceforward, every day is International Love Day.

some more very short stories

Sometimes I take myself too seriously. In my very short stories a spirit of whimsy tends to prevail.

Unhappy Planet

Once there was a planet on which everyone was un-
happy, except for one guy, who was terrifically happy.
"What's wrong with him?" everyone wondered.

Blue Sky

Once there was a blue sky with clouds in it.

Circus Adventure

Once there was a boy who wanted to run away and join the circus. But he didn't.

Man in a Hurry

Once there was a man who ate a sandwich without even tasting it.

Two Doughnuts

Once there were two doughnuts rolling down the road. One doughnut rolled into a puddle and started to disintegrate. His friend wanted to help, but what could he do? After all, he was just a doughnut.

(Or, the longer version):

Once there were two doughnuts rolling down the road. One doughnut rolled into a puddle and started to disintegrate. His friend wanted to help, but what could he do? After all, he was just a doughnut.

As he stood there watching his friend come apart, a crow flew down and picked him up in its beak and flew off. High in the air, held fast in the crow's beak, knowing he was not much longer for this world, the doughnut thought to himself: "We should have stayed back in the doughnut shop. Pete warned us not to go out into the wide world, which is full of dangers." (Pete was one of their doughnut friends.) The crow came in for a landing, far, he hoped, from any other crows. "Please, Mr. Crow, don't eat me!" said the doughnut. "Well, I'll be damned," the crow thought to himself, "a talking doughnut!" The crow paused for a moment—a talking doughnut might be worth a lot of money—then proceeded to gobble up the doughnut.

Meanwhile, miles away, back at the doughnut shop, Pete said to Al: (Al was another doughnut) "I wonder how the guys are doing. I hope they're okay." Just then, a policeman came into the doughnut shop…

The Adventurous Cheese

Once there was a cheese who didn't want to be a cheese. "Be thankful you are a cheese," his mother said, "and don't strive to be something you are not. Just stay in the refrigerator where it is safe and cool." But his mother's good advice fell on deaf ears. At the first opportunity the headstrong young cheese escaped from the refrigerator. A couple weeks later he returned, but he was almost unrecognizable. He had turned almost completely into mold and there was just a little orange part left in the middle. "Are you happy now?" his mother asked.

A Grasshopper and an Ant

Once there was a grasshopper and an ant. All summer long the grasshopper laughed and played, while the ant worked hard, storing food for the winter. "When winter comes you will have nothing to eat," the ant warned the grasshopper. But the grasshopper didn't heed the ant's warnings and went on his merry way.

One day, after the weather had turned cold, the ant was sitting inside his cozy home, telling stories to his kids before bedtime: "Once there was a man who sat watching TV by himself late at night," he began. "He was watching a show about a poor widower who had three sons. The oldest two were quite clever, but the youngest was a fool. The man gave them each a hundred bucks and told them to go forth and seek their fortunes. The oldest became a dentist. He married his beautiful dental hygienist. The two of them had a big house, nice cars, and two wonderful children.

The second son became a college professor. He married one of his bright and beautiful students. She was twenty years younger than him. They decided not to have children. Every summer they visited a different country!

The youngest son, who was not very bright, dropped out of school. He got low-paying jobs from time to time. They never lasted long. A friend of his turned him on to methamphetamines, of which he became quite fond. He ended up on the street: skinny, unwashed, raving out of his head.

The man turned off the TV. He was fed up with how stupid everything on TV is. He had an intense realization that the television was destroying his life. He opened a window, walked calmly over to the TV, unplugged it and proceeded to throw the TV out the window. The man lived on the fifth floor of an apartment building. The falling television killed a passerby."

"Is that the end of the story?" one of the little ants asked.

"Yes, it is," said the father. "Now go to sleep."

"What about the guy? Did he have to go to prison for throwing his TV out the window and killing a passerby?"

"I liked the story about the poor widower and his three sons," said another.

Just then there was a knock on the door. The ant got up to answer it. "Daddy, I'm thirsty. Can I have a glass of water?" one of the little ants asked. "Me too," said another. "Me too," chimed in a third.

"No. Now go to sleep." Despite further protestations, the ant made his way to the front door, and opened it. There stood the grasshopper. "Would you please give me some food?," the grasshopper asked.

"No," said the ant, "I won't," and shut the door.

A short time later there came another knock. The ant opened the door again. It was the grasshopper. "Get out of here," said the ant, and closed the door again.

The grasshopper went away and soon died. Not long after, the ant died, too.

Moral: Life is short.

The Nosepicking Man and His Wife

A man was picking his nose while walking down the street. A passing wag asked if he had found any jewels in the cave he was exploring. "No, just some boogers," replied the guileless man, "but then boogers were all that I had hoped to find in my nose. If I sought to find jewels, I would look in the ornately carved sandal-wood box that my wife keeps on her dresser." And the nosepicking man went on his way. Now the other man was a kind of rascal, and he went to the nosepicking man's house and rang the doorbell. The nosepicking man's wife answered the door in sheer sleep attire that left little to the imagination. "I'm taking a survey," the man hastily improvised. "May I come in and ask you a few questions?" The nosepicking man's wife saw through the man's ruse, but she invited him in anyway. She had been reading a torrid romance novel, and in her overheated imagination she was longing to be caught in the throes of an irresistible passion, which the nosepicking man—alas!—had not provided for quite some time. By a series of clever questions, the interloper, pretending that he was doing some kind of scientific research, got the woman to take off all her clothes and make passionate love to him. When she went to the bathroom, he took the opportunity to empty the sandalwood box of its precious jewels and put them in the pockets of his trousers. "I enjoyed taking part in your study," said the woman when she returned, "and I hope you will come back soon to do further research. But you must go now, before my husband comes home." And so the man went on his way, whistling a merry tune.

The Woman Who Imagined She Was Asleep

Once there was a woman who conceived the peculiar notion that she was asleep. Just as when we wake from sleep and open our eyes, a world comes into view, so, she imagined, she was supposed to wake up from the waking world to a world that was somehow more real. But how do you wake up from being awake? She had no idea. Still, she had a name for this imaginary world to which she felt she must awaken. She called it "The Golden World." The word "paradise" stirred a kind of yearning in her. But Paradise, she noted, was always somewhere else. There were legends that it had existed long ago. Other accounts held that one might go there after death. But this woman was not very imaginative, and it appeared to her that when you die you are dead. And the next thing that happens is: you begin to rot. At least this is what happens to animals that are hit by cars. It seemed to her that it must be the same for human animals.

As for the "soul," the word had never made any sense to her. Where was it? *What* was it? Some kind of intelligent, immortal gas? It made about as much sense to her as the idea of God as a kind of Cosmic Switchboard Operator who somehow could listen to millions of prayers at the same time. So, the idea of Paradise-after-you-die, which holds such promise for so many, held none for our protagonist.

As for the legends of earlier paradises, of Golden Ages, they seemed to her to be just that—legends! And yet she had an inkling that though they hadn't really, historically existed, maybe they were metaphors for something which could exist, or even does exist, if only you could wake from this sleep which people call waking life.

Her best surmise was that everyone around her was also sleeping. They seemed to be in the same predicament that she was, although they never mentioned feeling like they were asleep. But then, she never mentioned her feelings to anyone! Still, she had a strong intuition that this problem which obsessed her wasn't bothering anyone else that she knew.

There was something about babies! They seemed to be in a different world than the rest of us. Try as she might, she couldn't imagine what their world was like. Maybe they were in the Golden World, but couldn't say so. And by the time they learned to talk, they weren't in it any more.

"What exactly *is* waking life?," she wondered. We look at all these different things—but we don't just look. There's some sort of inner commentary that accompanies everything, that takes everything new and turns it into something old. It's as if when we wake up in the morning we turn on a little AM radio inside our head and it plays one inane thing after another, until, thankfully, we fall asleep at the end of our noisy day.

"I know," the woman thought to herself, "I'll try an experiment. I'll turn off the radio and see what the world looks like." But when she tried to turn off her inner radio, all she succeeded in doing was turning up the volume. It just about drove her nuts!

"Trying to wake up seems to be counterproductive," she concluded. "I don't try to wake up from sleep in the morning, I just wake up."

And then she woke up.

some more attempts

I keep trying.

How Hippies May Still Save the World

Shortly before the Era of Social Distancing began, my friend Bill Faricy and I were eating granola for breakfast and we got to thinking about hippies and what we have given to the world. Granola, for one. And whole wheat bread. Brown rice. Organic food. Recycling. Yoga. Vegetarianism. Holistic medicine. Natural childbirth and breastfeeding. Nonviolence. Massage. Bright colors! Free love. Good vibes. The list got longer and longer.

The most challenging problem that we humans face is that the way we are living is destroying the ecological health of our planet. Hippies intuited this, and began trying to live in harmony with Mother Earth. The changes were not just on the outside, with long hair and geodesic domes. There were deeper changes in thinking, feeling and imagining.

It was obvious that hippies were not going along with the status quo. The status quo is by its nature static, and resistant to change. The hippies clothing styles were mocked, but the peace symbol and the peace hand gesture—which are now emojis—represented something which threatened the foundation of an economy built on militarism and endless war.

The hippies laid-back attitudes were inimical to the Protestant ethic of Hard Work, and to the Spirit of Capitalism. Great efforts had been made and billions of dollars spent to turn citizens into Consumers and the hippies were opting out!—making their own sandals and growing their own food. At every turn the hippies weren't going along with The Program, and The Program was designed to create Endless Progress and Prosperity. What was wrong with them?

It turned out that there was something wrong with the global project of turning the planet into a Theme Park for Humans. The War On Nature is one we don't want to "win." The hippie chanteuse sang: "They paved Paradise and put up a parking lot."

I was born in 1951, and I didn't hear the word "ecology" before 1968. Around 1970, the year of the first Earth Day, it became evident to anyone who was curious and who read books that there were too many people on the planet for its "carrying capacity," and that we were not only cutting down all the trees and catching all the fish, but we were poisoning the world with our toxic chemicals and nuclear waste.

Hippies may have invented granola, and coined the expression "Have a nice day!," but most of the things on my list of contributions made by the hippies are older things that hippies revived and gave momentum to, like yoga, massage and good vibes. Hippies weren't the first vegetarians. Credit Buddha and Mahavira for that, about 500 BC, with their doctrines of nonviolence (*ahimsa*). Hippies didn't discover organic food. Before pesticides were invented, no one ate food with poison on it. And the alarm was sounded not by hippies, but by Rachel Carson—definitely a non-hippie scientist. But the hippies read her book *Silent Spring*, which was published in 1965, and started organizations like the Northwest Center for Alternatives to Pesticides.

Hippies started nonprofit organizations by the tens (or hundreds) of thousands. There are currently 1.5 million nonprofit corporations in the United States. I started two myself. There are an estimated 10 million non-governmental organizations (NGOs) in the world. Hippies didn't start them all—far from it!—but hippies are part of a long tradition of nonviolent revolutionary change from the bottom up.

"Hippies" is a word like "gypsies" that can refer to all kinds of people, all over the world. There is a caricatured picture of the long-haired, barefoot, stoned hippie that the mainstream media perpetuates. And surely there is a shadow side to hippie culture. I'm just giving one hippie's perspective on positive contributions that hippies have made, and how the Hippie Way of understanding and being-in-the-world can help us to make the transition to the Post Fossil Fuel Era as gently and beautifully as possible.

I don't want to convert anybody to Hippieism. I became a hippie effortlessly. I looked a certain way, dressed a certain way, and thought and acted in certain ways, and people pointed at me and said: "Look, Martha, a hippie!" I wrote an email to a woman in Lebanon in 2012 and signed it: "peace & love, Johnny." She knew I was a hippie.

My hair isn't long at present, and I only occasionally wear a hippie-style shirt from somewhere like Nepal or Africa or Guatemala. But I think like a hippie. I believe in Peace and Love—the core hippie values. I love Mother Earth and everyone who lives here—people, plants, animals, clouds, rivers, stones.

This subject is too big for this kind of short essay. Here are the most important hippie ideas:

Nature is Sacred
Money isn't Everything; (Money and Wealth are not the same thing)
Local Organic Agriculture
Local Economics
Community
Peace & Nonviolence
Children raised to be free, rather than obedient
Meditation & Mindfulness
Live the life you love; (Do your own thing)
Love Everyone!

I'm not going to elaborate on all these ideas, but I'll say a few more things. We can't continue to destroy the ecological health of the planet. Short term financial profit is not a good enough reason to do it. It's suicidal. And omnicidal.

One hundred years from now, food will be grown closer to where it is eaten. And most things we need will be made locally. The ecological damage inherent in large scale industrial production is unsustainable. The current economic system is unjust and inherently unstable. That which is unsustainable can't be sustained.

If all children were raised in a loving, nurturing environment, respected as people, allowed to realize their full human potential and follow their hearts' desires, our world would be transformed utterly. It's a tall order. To do it, adults will have to become more loving and kind. At present, at home and around the world, physical, psychological and emotional abuse of children is the norm. (See *For Your Own Good: Hidden Cruelty in Childrearing and the Roots of Violence* by Alice Miller.)

Meditation and mindfulness, which hippies were instrumental in helping to bring from the East to the West, can help us to co-create a Culture That Nurtures, a culture of Peace, Love, Happiness & Understanding.

We need to aspire to love everyone unconditionally. No exceptions. No enemies. No "others." One Human Family. It's easy! (Much easier than what we're doing now.) As Bob Marley sang:

One love!
One heart!

What Christmas Means to Me

It took me a long time to discover the error in presuming to write something with a title like "What Christmas Means." But I'm an authority on "What Christmas Means to Me." Who else?

It seems to me that every spoken or written sentence should begin with the phrase "it seems to me." But that would be tedious. I am not and you are not in a position to make pronouncements about the way things are.

Only Donald Trump is in that position. Just kidding.

And so, dear reader, don't take offense. This does not pretend to be the right way to look at Christmas. Just my way.

The birth of Jesus is a symbolic event, not a historical one. What it symbolizes is that every baby born on Planet Earth is an incarnation of the Divine.

End of essay. That's about all I've got to say on the subject, but I enjoy saying it.

Inner Work

What changes our inner landscape?

When I first attempted to meditate I became aware of how noisy it was inside my head. The thoughts wouldn't stop coming and I couldn't make them stop.

This morning, almost fifty years later, it's different. I'm awake and alert, but it's quiet inside. The world around me is beautiful.

In school we were taught to ignore each other and to take a keen interest in the doings of Dick and Jane and their dog Spot. When I was eight, a television arrived in our home. With it came the Cartwrights, the Flintstones and the Three Stooges.

The people inside the little box taught us to worry more. Did we have bad breath? Was bad weather on the way? Had we prepared adequately for our retirement?

Back in the day, we were told that the average 10 year old had witnessed something like 10,000 acts of violence on TV. Now, with video games, it must surely be 10,000 to the tenth power.

I was one of those hippies who went off to India to study with yogis. That might sound like the premise for a New Yorker cartoon, but I learned some things there for which I am grateful.

Just as the Jehovah's Witness comes to your door seeking to save your immortal soul, I would like to spread the good news of meditation and mindfulness.

Fortunately, I don't have to because, as my friend Howard points out, other people are already doing that.

There are many ideas about how we might improve ourselves. The Self Help section at Powell's bookstore is vast. Ironically, one of the titles is: *There is Nothing Wrong With You*. I'm in favor of self-help books. I'm in favor of anything that helps anyone.

Here's a little koan:

Two people sitting on a bench. One is happy. One is miserable. What's the difference?

What are, in William Stafford's phrase, "the little ways that encourage good fortune?"

What it feels like to be alive can vary radically from moment to moment, from day to day, and from person to person. What could be more important than whether we experience our life as a blessing or a curse?

Of course rich variety is intrinsic to human life. Sometimes we're happy, sometimes blue. As for me, I'm trying to live in a way whereby my life gets more wonderful as it goes along. Gradually, I want to become happier, kinder, wiser, more loving, more peaceful, more free.

It seems to be trending that way.

For which I am grateful.

The Missionary Position

When I was in second grade, the teacher asked us what we wanted to be when we grew up. I wrote "missionary" and drew a picture of a stick figure walking on top of a circle, which represented Planet Earth. My mom had been reading about Albert Schweitzer, and, suitably impressed, "missionary" is what popped into my mind when asked a question to which I probably hadn't given any thought.

In the 1950's, Albert Schweitzer was a famous saint, somewhat like Mother Teresa in more recent times. He had gone to "darkest Africa" and, in addition to saving souls, he had started a hospital, and played Bach on the organ. There was an article about him in Life magazine and he had written an autobiography, which my mom read. Okay, that's what I remembered just now about Albert Schweitzer. Looking him up on Wikipedia, I learn that he won the Nobel Peace Prize in 1952 for his philosophy of "Reverence for Life." He was a vegetarian!

I don't know anything about the "saving souls" aspect of his time in Africa, but he was definitely a "missionary," and that's what missionaries do. I have spent my adult life trying to not be such a missionary—that is, trying *not* to try to save the soul of everyone I meet. A deep-seated feature of my personality has been a desire to get other people to think like me, to know what I know, to believe what I believe. I'm not proud of this. Frankly, I'm ashamed of myself. If who we are consists of a whole cast of characters—a theory congenial to actors like me—then this aggressive member of the cast might be called Mr. Know-It-All.

Sometimes after one of my characteristically long-winded explanations, I think to myself: "That was him: Mr. Know-It-All"—and I feel abashed.

In my old age, I often find myself thinking: "What's the point?" What's the point of being "right"? And a lot of other things: What's the point of knowing stuff? What's the point of trying to gain a more adequate understanding of what's going on here? What's the point of sharing said understanding with other people? Sometimes I wonder: why read a book?, why go to a movie?, why do anything when you're going to die in the end? Another form this question takes is the ecological version: if the whole world is doomed, why bother trying to improve it, or save it, or whatever?

My temperament is such that I don't spend a lot of time in depression or despair. I have ways of answering those questions like "What's the point of anything?" in ways that work for me. For one thing, I don't want to spend a whole day of my precious human life on earth moping around. Here are some of the kind of things I might say to myself to cheer myself up and feel that my life is meaningful after all.

The universe may be incomprehensibly vast, and a

human life a blink of an eye in the history of the evolution of this little planet, but my life is meaningful to me. It's all I've got. My job is to enjoy it. To make the most of it. To live in love. To be free. To be kind. To enjoy feelings of peace and well-being. To be helpful to others when an occasion arises. To make things a little better—rather than a little worse—if I can. Maybe these things don't have significance on a cosmic scale. On a cosmic scale, maybe nothing has significance. Significance—meaning—is a human thing. So I prefer a human perspective to a cosmic one. And why shouldn't I? I'm a human being.

A lot of philosophical and intellectual talk is abstract and detached. It lacks *feeling*. It lacks love. But human beings have emotions. We need to love and be loved—whatever the scientists may or may not say about it. A whole human life is human—humane. If my life feels meaningful to me, it is meaningful. If I feel happy, I am happy. If I feel lucky, I am lucky. If I feel free, I'm free.

I'm not happy every moment of every day, but I'm slowly marinating in the hippie virtues of peace, love and happiness and it seems to be having an effect. People remark on it. My own subjective sense is that slowly, over time, I'm becoming more peaceful, loving, happy and free. Maybe if I gain enough confidence in my feeling of well-being, I will be able to come down off my soap box and join the picnic.

The Noble Ninefold Path

"If you have tears, prepare to shed them now," he said. We did and we did. The actor who was playing Marc Antony is 34 years old. He has spent the last 17 of those years in prison, which is where Nancy and I were watching this production of Julius Caesar. After the performance, the actors talked to the audience about how much they love each other, and tried to express how much that means to them "in a place like this."

I didn't direct this production, but in 2008 I directed a production of Hamlet at Two Rivers prison in Umatilla, Oregon, and have directed a number of plays in prison since then—mostly by William Shakespeare. For thirteen years I went to prison more-or-less every week and facilitated meaning-of-life dialogues. After doing this for a number of months, one day I mentioned the word "love." It's a word you are not supposed to say in prison. It is taboo outside of prison as well. But that's another story.

Inviting men in prison to talk about love had a strange effect. We all began to love each other. Over the years this love deepened to the point where we could all feel it. It was palpable.

I'm not the first person to notice this, but I've come to understand in a deep way that everyone needs to love and be loved. Like a puppy at the Humane Society, we are all waiting for someone to take us home.

What the men in prison taught me about living in love got me to thinking about how in philosophical traditions and in many spiritual traditions knowing is privileged over loving. I looked again at the noble eightfold path and it wasn't there. There was no mention of love!

I'm not a Buddhist and certainly not a scholar of Buddhism, but I realized something had to be done about this and so, with an utter lack of humility, I would like to suggest a revision to one of the Buddha's most fundamental teachings and propose to all and sundry the adoption of The Noble Ninefold Path:

right understanding
right thinking
right speech
right action
right living
right effort
right mindfulness
right meditation
right loving

This may sound like a joke, but it's not. I'm not suggesting that all the books on Buddhism be revised. What I'm suggesting is that if you use the noble eightfold path as a guide to your practice you could add one more thing to the list. And that it would be helpful to do so. It's not a trivial addition.

One could argue that the Mahayana tradition has already done something like this with the bodhisattva ideal of compassion for all beings. Fair enough. Many modern Buddhist teachers—I'm thinking at the moment of Thich Nhat Hanh, Pema Chödrön and Jack Kornfield—put a big emphasis on love. This idea of adding one more item to the eightfold path is done, I hope, in that same spirit.

Peace, love and happiness—the hippie virtues—all tend to be scoffed at by "smart people," maybe because these are arts which are not taught in school.

One meaning of nirvana is a kind of floating away from this world of cares—the world of samsara. But in later Buddhism, the duality is abolished: samsara and nirvana are not two.

For "intellectuals" and intellectual traditions the head is more important than the heart. This is not surprising. That's kind of what "intellectual" means. But it seems to me that being a whole human being is preferable to performing the role of Mr. Know-It-All. Love and understanding need each other.

Head without heart leads to tragedy. In my lifetime, a bunch of geniuses had all kinds of reasons why it was a good idea to drop jellied gasoline on families planting rice in paddies. Had they listened to their hearts, the whole thing could never have happened.

What is "right loving"? I don't know. Like all the other "rights" of the noble ninefold path, you do your best to figure it out as you go along. Love, of course, includes compassion. But love is much more than that. I love to see a beautiful flower. I don't feel compassion for it. I love it because it's beautiful. I love it without even knowing why I love it. Thich Nhat Hanh—that sweet man!—reminds us that we are all flowers.

My own aspiration is to love the heck out of everyone and every thing. "Unconditional love" means loving no matter what and for no reason.

In the Bible it says: "Who loves not, knows not God; for God is Love."

William Blake says:

Love to faults is always blind,
Always is to joy inclin'd,
Lawless, wing'd & unconfin'd,
And breaks all chains from every mind.

A good way to end this little essay might be with the Meta Prayer:

May all beings be happy!
May we be peaceful and at ease!
May we be well in body and mind!
May we live in love!

Peace, Love, Happiness
& Understanding in the Anthropocene

Dark days ahead. That's the forecast from Left, Right and Center. More importantly, that's the forecast from ecologists.

We are well into the Sixth Extinction, the Anthropocene. If you don't know what that means, you have some reading to do. In this essay, I'm not going to try to convince the "unbelievers." I'm relying upon the scientists, who tell us that there are way too many human beings on this planet for it's "carrying capacity," which means that the forests, the topsoils and the "fisheries" have been relentlessly depleted to feed an ever-expanding human population. In addition to which, the burning of fossil fuels is changing the climate in ways that make living here much more difficult for humans and for many species of plants and animals.

Hopefully, by now, you have a pretty good grasp of the situation. The question arises: What can we do? There are many practical answers to this question which include things like solar power and wind generators. It would be good if we could reduce the human population without violence, in ways that are rational and fair. Many changes could, in theory, be legislated. Much is known about what could be done. And much is known about the countervailing forces, including

Corporate Capitalism and its formidable campaign of disinformation and propaganda.

The future is unknown. This is axiomatic. For the purposes of this essay, let's assume that the forces for and against the status quo are in a kind of stalemate and that things will tend to go in the direction they are going—increasing human population, deforestation, plant & animal extinction, climate change—until various kinds of collapses ensue: political, economic, social, technological. Certainly not a happy scenario, but, also, not an altogether far-fetched one.

That this may happen does not mean that all efforts toward, for example, passing the necessary legislation should not be vigorously pursued in order to minimize the suffering that will inevitably take place during the transition to the post-fossil fuel era. Suffering cannot be abolished. There has always been, is now, and will always be suffering.

Whether things get "better" or get "worse," there will always be more than enough suffering and plenty for anyone to do who wants to do good deeds. Some suffering can be prevented by wise compassionate action. Some wounds can be healed. Some wrongs can be forgiven or forgotten. Maybe the most important preparation for "the future"—whatever it may bring—is to nurture loving community. In good times and bad we need each other. We need to love and be loved.

Each one of us can live in love right now. We don't need to wait for war or injustice to end. We should do what we can to promote peace and justice. A good beginning is to deepen our inner peace. The Golden Rule is a pretty good guide to moving in the direction of a more just world: Do unto others as you would have them do unto you.

The Golden Rule. It's an old idea. I'm all for better electric cars, but mostly what we are going to need in The Anthropocene (i.e. Right Now) is loving community—more peace, love, happiness and understanding.

My Recipe for Living a Life Rich in Meaning

Beginning My Studies

Beginning my studies the first step pleas'd me
so much,
The mere fact consciousness, these forms, the
power of motion,
The least insect or animal, the senses, eyesight,
love,
The first step I say awed me and pleas'd me so
much,
I have hardly gone and hardly wish'd to go any
farther,
But stop and loiter all the time to sing it in
ecstatic songs.

—Walt Whitman

What I would like to do in this essay is to provide some clues as to how to find your way to the Golden World, and live there. This is *my* recipe. You have to create your own. That's part of the fun. Make the most of the fact that there has never been and will never be another you.

To live a life rich in meaning, the first thing is to have that as an aspiration. A much more common goal in our society is simply to get rich. Rich in money and rich in meaning are not the same thing. My basic idea is: Since life is short and each day is precious, I want to BLESS THIS DAY.

There is not some other day to be happy. Today is the day.

Some of the ingredients that make my life rich in meaning include: love, silence, books, friends, creativity, gratitude, and being helpful to others.

We all need to love and be loved. One of my constant aspirations is to become a more loving person. We learn to love by loving and being loved. I have the extreme good fortune to be living with Nancy, who loves me and who I love. We've been living together for 17 years. We're nuts about each other. Every day together is a good day.

Nancy and I got together when I was 55 years old. Since I was single at the time, it means that all of my previous efforts to be in a loving relationship had not worked out, and yet I learned a lot about loving from each of them.

There is also Big Love—unconditional love for everyone and everything. Being in a loving relationship is one aspect of living in love. It nurtures and strengthens the heart muscle and the bigger project of loving everyone, of loving life. I don't know exactly how or why it worked out this way, but having a three-hour meaning-of-life dialogue every week for many years with a dozen or more friends in prison did a lot to open my heart. It made me softer. I cry more than most men do. In those prison circles, we opened ourselves to each other. This gave everyone in the circle many blessings. We humans need each other more than we know. Our potential for loving has no limit.

Peace is something that is not given much attention in our society. By "peace" I mean here "inner peace"—what the Bible calls "the peace which passeth understanding." My introduction to peace as a value to aspire to came from Indian yogis. First from books by J. Krishnamurti and Paramanhansa Yogananda, then from spending time with two teachers I had when I was in my twenties, Nataraja Guru and Nitya Chaitanya Yati.

Meditation and mindfulness are essential ingredients in my recipe for living a life rich in meaning—the most essential. I can't imagine what my life would be like without them. More miserable, for sure. They provide the foundation for whatever peace and love and happiness and freedom I have. It feels to me like I have a lot of those things. Every day of my life is filled with blessings. As I look around, everything appears miraculous to me. I am thankful for my human life on earth.

My Paradise is a library. I live surrounded by books. Each one is a world. Some of the authors and even some of the fictional characters are among my closest friends. I love Walt Whitman and Alice, who has adventures in Wonderland and through the Looking-Glass. I hated school. As soon as I dropped out of college, I began to read whatever I wanted to. I read widely, going from subject to subject and author to author as the mood strikes me. I get endless pleasure from this. As for living a life rich in meaning, there is no building more packed with meaning, from floor to ceiling, than a library. My own library contains a lot of books by people who are especially good on the subject of living a meaningful life. Some of my favorites, to whom, I return again and again, include: Thich Nhat Hanh, Susan Griffin, Joseph Campbell, Wendell Berry, Walt Whitman, J. Krishnamurti, Alan Watts, Hafiz, William Shakespeare, Ramana Maharshi, Shunryu Suzuki, Lao Tzu, Thomas Traherne, Ralph Waldo Emerson, John Moriarty and Han Shan. It's a much longer list, but these are some of the people whose writings most reliably enrich my life.

Friends enrich my life. If I look at my life, it appears that my vocation is gathering people together. For many years, I would make waffles at my house (or apartment) every Sunday and have somewhere around 20 people come over. For thirteen years I had a weekly dialogue group at a prison with around 16 people sitting in a circle and talking about—guess what!—how to live a life rich in meaning. The original title of the dialogue group was: The Stories We Tell Ourselves: How Our Thinking Shapes Our Lives. I love this kind of deep dialogue. I like to get together with friends for coffee or tea—often one-on-one—and talk about everything under the sun, but especially about what is most important, or essential, or meaningful to us in that moment. During the pandemic, I hosted a lot of Zoom gatherings. Now we have a greater appreciation of how wonderful it is to be in each other's presence.

There are many well-worn roads of religious belief and practice that one might go down, but the only way I know through first-hand experience is to create your own path by following your heart's desire. I suspect that even if one chooses one of those well-travelled roads, each person must find their own unique way of knowing, believing and practicing that tradition.

In addition to religious belief and practice, some people live lives rich in meaning by devoting themselves to Art: theater, music, poetry, dance, painting—not to mention other arts, like gardening, cooking, wood-working, knitting, filmmaking, et cetera. My friend Abe goes hiking, skiing and camping in the Montana wilderness. He takes beautiful photos of some of the things he sees. He reports that his journeys give him great joy.

Creativity enriches our lives in mysterious ways. Theater is a realm in which I have had many adventures, as an actor and director. I haven't given myself fully to an art form in the way that some of my art heroes have: Bill T. Jones, Ushio Amagatsu, Peter Schumann, Wes Anderson, Tom Waits, Susan Griffin, Rick Bartow—to name a few. One of my current role models is the fictional character Ted Lasso. I want to be more like him!

I've done some writing, and would like to do more. I've written some essays, poems, short stories and theater pieces. I've kept a journal for fifty years. The journal has helped me to better understand my life journey. I also use it as a tool to help me find my way to the Golden World every morning.

Helping others is another thing that enriches our life and gives meaning to it. Life is short. It often seems to me that the world's problems are large, I am puny, and whatever I do won't make much of a difference in the Big Picture. One of the things I tell myself when I'm having those thoughts, is that one kind act makes a whole life worthwhile. Everyone enjoys being helpful, when an opportunity arises. I know some people who don't wait—they are always finding ways to help someone. I'm thinking of Brenda Erickson, Dick Willis, Jude Russell and Jack Baird. Bodhisattvas all!

Following your heart's desire may sound selfish, but it's important to distinguish between selfishness and self-care. I have often reminded my friends in prison that self-care is Job One. I remind them of this when they get out of prison, for there are many challenges outside prison walls as well. Because our life is short and each day is precious, we should be able to bless each day—to be thankful that we have a human life on earth. That's another not-so-secret ingredient in my recipe for living a life rich in meaning: gratitude. At the most basic level, the difference between complaining and giving thanks is the difference between Hell and Heaven.

Which brings me to another important thing that I wanted to include in my recipe—coming to understand that every day, from moment to moment, we create the world in which we live. The stories we tell ourselves *are* our world. It's important to distinguish between *the* world and *my* world, as Wittgenstein pointed out long ago. *The* world includes everything that has ever happened, and everything that is happening right now. It is beyond our ken, not only because it is so vast, but because it is changing from moment to moment. *My* world is the world as I experience it and understand it and know it and feel it, from moment to moment. At times, I may feel powerless to change *the* world, but I can be sovereign of my inner world and how I process my experience. A happy person lives in a friendly world. An angry person lives in a world full of assholes. A person who lives in love, lives in love.

This is not to deny or minimize, even for a moment, the vast amount of injustice and suffering that is always going on in *the* world. Right now, there are many places in our world where food is scarce and machine guns are plentiful. This is not acceptable, since all children are our children. Each of us must do what we can to make this world a better place for all our human, animal and plant friends, for all the rivers and forests and ecologies of every kind.

Peace and love and joy and freedom and gratitude and beauty and wisdom are all intrinsically good for us. Where self-care comes in is by nurturing these qualities in ourselves, so that we can bring them to every encounter we have with each other, with all beings, and with our Mother Earth.

Well, that's about what I've got this morning as far as a recipe goes for living a life rich in meaning. I have a very limited repertoire. Apologies to my friends who have heard me say all this before.

July, 2006

July of 2006 might have passed uneventfully for many people. For me it was a life-changer. Three Big Things happened. I met Jerry Smith. I started facilitating meaning-of-life dialogues at Two Rivers prison in Umatilla, Oregon. And I got together with Nancy Scharbach.

It's weird. I don't know how or why these life-altering events happened at the same time. I was 55. Destined, it seemed, to live out my life as a dharma bum—reading, feeding the birds, practicing coffee shop philosophy.

I was living in Ashwood, Oregon. The population fluctuated from time to time. It averaged about 12 people and eight horses. I was Assistant Postmaster, which meant that once in a while I would fill in for Lanell and spend 4 hours selling a few stamps, if anyone happened to come in. There was no gas station or store in Ashwood. Stamps were the only thing you could buy.

I earned some money performing my solo version of King Lear and other theatrical oddities in various places, mostly in Portland, which was a three-hour drive.

I had squandered most of what was left of my modest inheritance on a homesteader's cabin. I purchased it for $25,000 from the aforementioned Nancy Scharbach, and lived there from July of 2003 to July of 2006.

My life has happened to me. I haven't planned anything.

Nancy was once married to my friend Peter Clough. I knew him quite well—I worked with him in the Maintenance Department of the Parry Center, which was a home for emotionally disturbed kids—but I hardly knew Nancy at all.

Some years prior to 2003, Peter invited me to come with them to their cabin in Ashwood. I loved it there! I asked if I could use the cabin sometimes when they weren't there. They said "okay," and I would go out there often, staying a few days, or a week. It was so peaceful! It felt like a kind of paradise to me.

Peter and Nancy broke up, then got divorced. About a year after their divorce, Peter told me that Nancy was planning to sell the cabin. "I'll buy it!," I said. And I did.

A few months later, I quit my job in Portland and moved into the cabin in Ashwood. I lived there for three years. It was a happy time for me. One day, there was a knock on the door. That didn't happen very often. It was Nancy, who was camping in Central Oregon with her brother Johnny. She says that she thought her brother would enjoy talking with me.

They camped in Ashwood for a couple nights. We visited in my kitchen. I made chai and my usual un-imaginative vegetarian meals. We all talked a lot. I liked Nancy's brother Johnny, but I *really* liked Nancy. We began emailing, then dating, then she invited me to live with her in Portland. "Free haircuts for life!," she said.

We recently celebrated our 17th anniversary. We're not married, but that's how long we've been a couple. We are happy together. We don't quarrel. Every day is a good day. Some people say that "relationships are a lot of work." Not this one. It's easy. Imagine the way a golden retriever greets its person. Always right there at the front door with tail wagging. It's like that for both of us.

In 2005, a Jefferson County Commissioner organized a trip to the nearest prison, which was three hours away. She thought it would be good for local citizens to see what a prison is like, since one was being built in Jefferson County, near Madras. I was curious.

The prison surprised me. Very friendly, well-educated administrators gave us the tour. The prison was clean. It struck me that prison is a kind of social service agency—which it is. I offered to do a performance there. They said, "Okay." My friend Howard Thoresen gave me some money so that I could perform my solo version of King Lear at the prison. I did two performances. After each performance I had wonderful conversations with the men who came to see the play. They invited me back.

Six months later, I performed a piece about meditation called "Silence." The post-show conversations were even better this time! One of the men said he was reminded of the conversations that Socrates had in ancient Athens. I said, "You could have this kind of conversation without me." Another man said, "I hate to burst your bubble, but we can't. We aren't allowed to 'congregate' in groups of more than six, which is how we eat. To do this, someone from the outside has to come—someone like you." I said I'd think about it.

After another six months passed, I performed my solo version of Hamlet at Two Rivers prison. Again the dialogue after the show was amazing. Again the prison residents invited me to come back. I enjoyed all my prison conversations so much that I decided I would teach a class there.

A short time later, after a performance of Hamlet in Portland, a man came up to me and asked about how the play went in prison. I said it went well, and that I was now planning to teach a class there. He said, "Maybe I can help." I thanked him, but said that I was planning to get money from foundations to do it. He said, "I have a foundation. How much do you want?" That was how I met Jerry Smith, and how I was able to begin doing weekly meaning-of-life dialogues at Two Rivers prison—"The Stories We Tell Ourselves: How Our Thinking Shapes Our Lives."

I started a nonprofit organization, Open Hearts Open Minds, and went inside Oregon prisons more-or-less every week for 13 years. After doing the weekly dialogue group for two years, one of the men, who was serving a life sentence, asked if I would like to do a play with them. I directed a production of Hamlet at Two Rivers prison in 2008. It was the first time men in an Oregon prison had performed a play by Shakespeare. Nancy did the costumes and props for the play, and helped the men learn their lines.

Nancy and I worked as a team on seven plays at Two Rivers prison. We had a lot of fun doing that. A lot of the actors have graduated from prison. We stay in touch with them. Some of them have begun doing theater "on the outside."

I'm very grateful to Jerry Smith, his wife Donna, their daughters Marsha and Chris, and their grandson Jordon for their love and support for all of my projects—inside and outside of prison—since the fateful day in July of 2006 when Jerry uttered that memorable understatement: "Maybe I can help."

July of 2006 happened seventeen years ago for most people. It's still happening for me.

The Incommensurability of Everything

The idea that we might know who we are or what's going on here is preposterous, when you think about it.

another poem

Too long to be a small poem.

wake up, heart!

wake up, heart!

wake up and love everyone and every thing

love the unlovable

the unhappy old men who start the wars

the geniuses who collapse the economy

the heads of the big corporations who ruin the earth

they need love, too

why else would they do stuff like that?

we all want to love and be loved

we all need to love and be loved

love everything that moves

and everything that won't budge

love the person who is reading or listening to this poem

you might start with the easy ones

passing dogs

laughing children

fluffy white clouds

all the spring flowers shouting "love me!"

practice on the easy ones

until you get so good at it that you accidentally love
the weird and scary homeless people, the criminals,
the people whose views differ from yours—before you
have time to think about it

heart, you were born for love

mr. brain sometimes tells you not to

"don't love that one," he says, "that one doesn't de-
serve it"

"don't be a fool"

forgive mr. brain

he can't help it

he's always making distinctions between this and that

he needs a hug

you know better

you know that the thing to do is just to love

to wake up and love without limit

another theater piece

I've never performed this. I'm not sure it really qualifies as a theater piece. Here it is anyway.

The Golden World

where is the golden world?
it's right here

what is it?
it's a place of quiet joy
a place where everything is miraculous

i know i'm in the golden world
when there is nowhere i would rather be

the golden world is paradise
not the paradise that existed long ago

or the paradise that is yet to come

but this one

to get to the golden world
one thing that sometimes helps
is to slow down

rushing around
trying to get somewhere else
we fail to appreciate where we are

when this ordinary world is alive for us
with beauty, with joy, with love, with peace
we are in the golden world

this ordinary world is the golden world
transformed by a shift in the way we see it
or feel it

one of the most astonishing things about us
is our ability to take things for granted
we get used to trees, to the sky, to birds
to each other
to ourselves
to life as we live it

we are just here a little while
we better wake up right now

we are always in the golden world
but when we imagine it is somewhere else
we feel that we are in exile

hoping we will somehow improve
wishing things were different
we miss the blessings we have
the blessings of who we are

a goldfinch doesn't imagine that it can improve

there is suffering within us and around us
the remedy for the suffering within us is close at hand

as for the big world
it is always simultaneously full of great suffering
and great beauty

if we do not live in quiet joy
in beauty, in truth
in freedom, in love—
what i am calling the golden world—
we cannot transform the suffering

of course, some suffering is built into the world
we are mortal creatures
disease and death are inevitable

but there is gratuitous suffering
we create through our ignorance,
our hatred, our anger, our fear

if we imagine we have an enemy
we are always at war

our inner conflict is the source of much outer conflict
wars begin in the minds of men

there is a stillness
in which there is no conflict
we can live there
or here
in the golden world

the peace which passeth understanding
is our birthright
maybe we forgot
got lost

it's time to remember
to come home
to the golden world

we are born into the golden world
we learn to understand and to speak a language
it's an astonishing thing!

we create an identity, a story about who we are
we create a mythos, a story about the world in which
     we live
these are fantastic achievements!

but, alas!, these stories become the prisons in which
     we live
we take everything new and turn it into something old

we don't live in the world
we live inside our descriptions of the world

we are fictional characters
living in fictional worlds of our own creation

the golden world is this ordinary world
not mediated by thought or language

we touch it all the time
whenever we take a sip of tea
and are not doing anything but taking a sip of tea
we are in the golden world

a quiet setting makes it easier for us to experience the
    golden world
but when the stillness is strong within us
the whole noisy world is golden

when thought and language are our tools
rather than our masters
they are a blessing
not a curse

when meditation is not just something we do for half-
    an-hour in the morning
when we live in meditation
we live in the golden world

we are always in the golden world
whether we know it or not
the place we've always wanted to get to
is where we are

that which is not born
and does not die
is who we are

in the golden world
there is nothing to strive for
no regret

all our sins are washed away

the golden world is not an imaginary place
the world described in the newspaper is an imaginary
    place

the golden world is never somewhere else
it is always right now where we are
or not at all

when you are in it
you are not

when you can't see it
you are blind

when the poet said
"each moment and whatever happens thrills me with joy"
he was in it
and when he said
"Divine am I inside and out,
and I make holy whatever I touch
or am touch'd from"

when another poet felt that he "was blessed
and could bless"
he was in it

another poet clarified the matter when she said:
"The Infinite a sudden Guest
Has been assumed to be—
But how can that stupendous come
Which never went away?"

you can't get to the golden world by trying to go there
when you are not trying to go somewhere
not trying to do something
not trying to be someone
you might find that you are in the golden world

when i'm in it, i think
"this is my home
i must never allow myself to lose this
even for a moment"

then, later, it's gone
did i leave the golden world?
or did it leave me?

i find myself in exile
and want to return

i know that that wanting condemns me to exile
and so i seek to find my way home by a kind of
    indirection
instead of doing something
i do nothing

when the mind is quiet and alert
it doesn't matter whether "i" am in the golden world
    or not
the question doesn't arise
or if it does
it is seen for what it is

the squirrel outside, sitting on a branch
has no ideas about a golden world
and so it lives in the golden world

"the golden world" is a name i give to something
that has no name

to have an identity is to be in exile

am i in the golden world?
or is the golden world in me?

behind each person's mask
shines a radiant, glorious, perfect being

beneath who we pretend to be
is who we are

at those moments when we see through everyone's mask
we are in the golden world

when we see through someone's mask
it is impossible not to love them

for this to be paradise
we have to love everyone
without love, it isn't paradise

when where we are
and where we want to be
are the same place
we are in the golden world

the seer sees the golden world
the seeker seeks the golden world
the seeker asks: where is it?
the seer replies: where isn't it?

this is it

you want a miracle?
the poet said:
"a mouse is miracle enough to stagger sextillions of
    infidels"
if that is so
where can you find something that is not miraculous?

there has never been
is not now
and will never be
anything more perfect
more beautiful
more miraculous
than a glass of water

there are miracles everywhere you look
the eyes with which we see
are miraculous

our brains, nervous systems
our heart's pumping blood
miracles!

that we are alive

and aware
in this world of marvels
is a great blessing

one last small poem

A "sangha" is a spiritual community.

my sangha

all people, plants, animals
clouds, stones, rivers
imaginings

Appendix

from *Encyclopædia Jonnica*

Encylopædia Jonnica is a heretofore unpublished compendium of my thoughts on various topics. I don't expect you, dear reader, to agree with all my oddball ideas. It would be kind of disappointing if you did. These are some of the shorter entries.

Animism. The crazy idea that everything is sacred.

Art of Happiness. One of the Arts not taught in school. Happiness is the art of not making yourself miserable.

Art of Living. One of the Arts not taught in school. The secret of the art of living is to follow your heart's desire.

Art of Loving. One of the Arts not taught in school. The first thing is to aspire to love everyone unconditionally, without exception. While you're at it, why not include all plants, animals, stones, rivers, clouds? If you engage fully with life and with all kinds of people, your heart will get broken many times. The broken heart is tender, permeable. Feelings can get in and out of a broken heart. A soft-hearted person's cheeks are frequently moistened by tears.

Center of the World. Where you are standing.

Childrearing. At Powell's bookstore there are three sections that give advice about how to raise children: Parenting, Education and Child Psychology. In each section, there are basically two approaches. One is: how to train children to be obedient, to do what you want them to do, to be well-behaved. The other is something like: how to help your child realize her or his fullest potential. Training children to obedience through fear is a great way to create a society of slaves and robots. Wilhelm Reich said that the authoritarian family is the training ground for the authoritarian state.

Complaining. The art of making a bad situation worse. A bad mental habit. If persisted in, it leads to the conclusion that life sucks.

Cultural Junk Food. Activities, ideas, entertainment that do not nourish us. I'm going to go out on a limb and, at the risk of sounding cranky, make a short list of some things that might fall into this category: death metal, slasher movies, horror movies, zombie apocalypse movies, video gaming, watching TV, gambling, boxing, mixed martial arts, car racing, drug addiction, pornography, smoking cigarettes. You can make your own list.

Gratitude. Antidote to complaining. When we practice gratitude, it helps us to appreciate what a blessing it is to live a human life on Earth.

Identity. Thanks to thought and language, and with the help of our family and our culture, we create an identity, a "constructed self," as we grow up. It is a collection of stories, images, ideas and descriptions of who we are. We also create a mythos—a collection of stories about the world and our place in it. We get stuck with our identity: woman, man, Republican, fat, depressed, Japanese, beatnik, Johnny—whatever. It is necessary to have an identity to function in the world, but it becomes a kind of prison. We tend to imagine that it is *who we are*. Alan Watts spoke and wrote a lot about the error of imagining ourselves to be a "skin-encapsulated ego," separate from and at war with each other and with Nature. It is good to practice seeing through these fictions, to spend some time in silence. Thich Nhat Hanh's idea of interbeing can be helpful in this regard.

Interbeing. A beautiful word, coined by Thich Nhat Hanh to describe the way things are. He gives the example of the pages of a book. They come from trees, which are nourished by soil and water and sunshine. A flower, he says, is made entirely of "non-flower elements." So, too, with us. Each breath of air sustains our life.

Local Economy. A "global economy" puts everyone at the mercy of large, precarious forces beyond our control. Economies periodically collapse. Healthy small-scale local economies, combined with local agriculture would be wonderful things to bequeath to our children and their children.

Map of Oregon. In order for a map of Oregon to contain everything in Oregon, it would have to be Oregon. Another problem with representing Oregon is that things are constantly changing. Plants are growing, birds are flying from place to place. It's very hard to keep track of all the ants. The width of Oregon changes as the tide ebbs and flows. All descriptions and explanations are partial. They simplify what is. They leave things out. The world cannot be known. It is beyond our ken. We need maps as aids to navigation on our life journey. Some maps are better than other maps. A map of Oregon shaped like a pineapple would not be very helpful.

Miracles. Everything, without exception, is miraculous.

My Mythos. In the first part of life, a lively exploration, following your curiosity, your inspiration, your desires. During this first phase, we create an identity, a constructed self—stories about who we are. We also create a mythos—stories about the world and our place in it. The next step is to find *moksha*, freedom, through spiritual practices, like meditation and mindfulness, and through philosophical inquiry. The idea here is to come to a clear understanding that one's constructed self and worldviews are fictions. Last phase (maybe) is to embrace our humanness, our idiosyncratic life on earth, our emotions, personality and unique life journey. My aspiration is to love everyone, to live in peace, to continually improve my understanding of what's going on here, to be happy, to be free, to be kind.

My World and *The* World. In the *Tractatus*, Ludwig Wittgenstein talks about this. *My* world is the world as I experience and imagine it, from moment to moment. *The* world is an abstraction. All descriptions of *the* world are partial, as *the* world is too big to be described. Such descriptions are distorted and lopsided, in spite of their pretense of accuracy. Some descriptions and explanations are more adequate than others—our planet is more like a ball than a pancake. We get some of our pictures of *the* world from The New York Times, and from television. Yikes! *The* world is everything-at-once: beyond our ken. As for *my* world—the world of my experience—it changes from moment to moment. A happy man lives in a friendly world. An angry man lives in a world of assholes.

Mythos. I use the word "mythos" to mean the stories we tell ourselves about the world and our place in it.

Our mythos might be patriotic, progressive, compassionate, fearful, optimistic. It may include religious beliefs, strong political views, et cetera. Our stories change over time. From moment to moment, we live in the world we imagine. It can be a paradise or a hell realm.

Nonstop Love-In. What our human life on Earth can be. Or is.

Paradise. There are stories that Paradise existed long ago. Some people dream of a Paradise yet to come on earth or in heaven. This beautiful planet is already a Paradise. We humans often create suffering for ourselves and each other, but at any moment you or I can feel perfect peace, love, joy—Paradise!

Prison. For thirteen years I facilitated a weekly three-hour-long dialogue circle in Oregon prisons. What I learned by doing this is that people in prison are not different from people who are not in prison. Everyone, without exception, has something perfect and beautiful at the core of who they are. Deep dialogue with men and women in prison broke my heart and, through a mysterious alchemy, made me a more loving person.

Spirituality. Like religion, in a way, but broader. A sense of the sacredness of all life, without creeds. The spiritual dimension of life can be equated with depth and with meaning.

Johnny Stallings. A fictional character. As Shakespeare said: "All the world's a stage, and all the men and women merely players." I spend a certain amount of time pretending to be Johnny Stallings. If I don't, who will? A lot of the time, though, I feel no such responsibility or obligation.

Stillness. Awake and alert, when thought and language fall away, a lovely state of serenity ensues, for which there is no boundary. Indescribable.

Stories. As we grow up, we hear stories. We tell ourselves stories. We tell stories to each other. These include the kind of stories that are found in storybooks and novels, as well as stories about who we are and about what's going on here. All stories are fictions—including scientific ones. That is not a bad thing. Imagination is one of our most wonderful gifts! Still, it's good to remind oneself with some frequency that all stories are stories. Some stories are toxic, like ones about "inferior races." Other stories are beneficial, like the ones which tend to promote peace, love, happiness and understanding.

War Against Nature. Of all the wars, maybe the dumbest.

About the Author

My Life So Far

I'm enjoying my human life on Earth!

Kay Stallings gave birth to me on August 17, 1951, in Whitefish, Montana. Bill Stallings was my dad. I have a sister, Mary Wallace, who is four years older than me. Our family moved from Columbia Falls, Montana to Portland, Oregon when I was eight. When I was a kid, I loved to play. I hated school.

When I was in high school, the prospect of getting drafted into the military and being sent to Vietnam loomed large. I didn't want to do that. I read black writers like Martin Luther King, Malcolm X and Dick Gregory, who had a critique of America. They wrote about genocide against indigenous peoples, slavery and the terrible war in Vietnam. By the time I graduated from high school, I was a committed pacifist.

I'm a hippie. My hair, once long, is shorter now, but the hippie era shaped my sensibilities in many ways. I believe in the hippie values of peace & love. A classic hippie phrase is: "Do your own thing." I've have done, and continue to do, my own thing.

In 1969, the Summer I graduated from Maui High School, I read *On the Road* and *The Dharma Bums* by Jack Kerouac. In my twenties, I hitchhiked around a lot, and became a dharma bum. By the spring of 1970,

I had already dropped out of Portland State University. I never liked school. It took me a while to realize that after high school, school is optional. I opted out. That's when my education began in earnest. I read whatever I wanted to read! To this day, I carry five or six books with me wherever I go. My life feels like a dream in which I wandered into The Library and got lost. I live surrounded by books.

In the Summer of 1970 I read *The Autobiography of a Yogi* by Paramahansa Yogananda. That book was a window on a world I didn't know existed. I wanted to get the kind of peace that yogis have. I started meditating.

In the Fall of 1971 I met a real swami from India, Nitya Chaitanya Yati. I became his student and went to India. I spent a year with his teacher, Nataraja Guru. It was the last year of Nataraja Guru's life. I was Nitya's student for ten years. I learned a lot from these two men. I'm grateful that I spent my twenties studying with yogis, instead of going to Vietnam to kill people.

I cherish the time I spent with my gurus. Breaking off my relationship with Nitya was for me a momentous decision. It was a door to greater freedom. Like my lifelong companion Walt Whitman, I realized that sacredness is everywhere, in everyone. In my early forties, more than twenty years after I began meditating, I finally got the hang of inner stillness, where thought and language fall away. I got what I went to India to get.

For many years, when people asked me "What do you do?" I would say: "I'm an actor." I've read plays, seen plays, seen films based on plays, written plays, acted in plays and directed plays. In Shakespeare's day, I would have been called "a player." That means something different now.

The year 2006 was a big one for me. Nancy Scharbach and I became a happy couple. We still are. That same Summer I began doing meaning-of-life dialogues at Two Rivers prison in Eastern Oregon. Two years later, Nancy and I began doing plays with the men in the dialogue group. Our friend Bushra Azzouz made a documentary film about our 2010 production: "A Midsummer Night's Dream in Prison." The film premiered in Portland on August 7, 2022.

I'm currently the Executive Director of The Open Road, which is a learning community. Looking back on my life so far, it seems that my vocation is to gather people together. I used to have twenty or thirty people over for waffles every Sunday. This went on for years! I've spent more time in coffee shops and tea shops than anyone else in history. You can look it up in the Guinness Book of World Records.

I think of my life as The Nonstop Love-In.

Printed in the USA
CPSIA information can be obtained
at www.ICGtesting.com
CBHW072021120324
5289CB00001B/2